THE IRISH GRANNY'S
pocket
BREAD &
BAKING
BOOK

Gill Books
Hume Avenue, Park West, Dublin 12

www.gillbooks.ie

Gill Books is an imprint of M.H. Gill & Co.

ISBN: 978-0-7171-7292-4

This book was created and produced by Teapot Press Ltd

Recipes compiled by Fiona Biggs
Designed by Tony Potter
Picture research and photography by Ben Potter
Home economics by Christine Potter

Printed in Europe

This book is typeset in Garamond and Dax

A CIP catalogue record for this book is available
from the British Library.

5 4 3 2 1

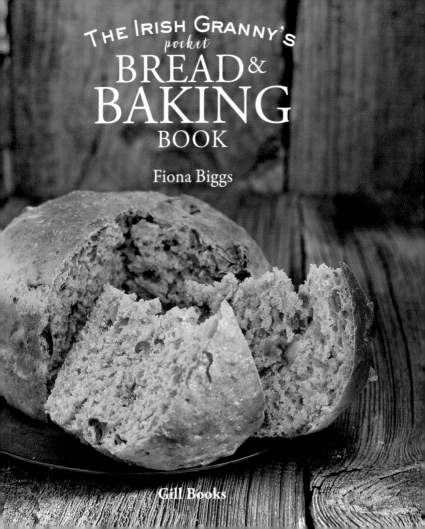

The Irish Granny's *pocket*
BREAD &
BAKING
book

Fiona Biggs

Gill Books

Contents

19th C. Farmhouse, Co Antrim

Introduction

Baking is one of the most satisfying types of cooking there is – it fills the house with comforting aromas and the anticipation of wholesome and delicious baked treats. There's something about baking as an activity that is very therapeutic, whether it's kneading dough for the perfect loaf of bread, rustling up a batch of biscuits or creating a favourite cake for a special family occasion.

The Irish baking tradition might seem to be confined to the delicious breads, bracks and oatcakes that could be made over an open fire using a bastible or griddle. Yeast was not readily available to early bakers and would have been difficult to use in cooking vessels that had no temperature regulation. Bread was hearty and substantial rather than light and airy, biscuits were wholesome and sweet cakes (frequently laced with alcohol) were a very occasional treat. However, in the big houses, which had large range-type ovens, kitchens turned out bread, cakes and baked desserts that could rival those of any establishment in Britain or Europe.

The advent of domestic electrification in the 1950s and 1960s, coupled with a steady emigration from Ireland to the US, brought about a minor revolution in Irish kitchens. Recipes sent home from abroad for sweet bakes such as cheesecake, carrot cake and lemon meringue pie have been popular in Ireland for decades, and we've made some recipes our own with the addition of specifically Irish ingredients, such as Irish cream liqueur. People who had served in the kitchens of the big houses inherited recipes for British classics such as Victoria sponge (see page 70), Bakewell tart (see page 168) and queen cakes (see page 202), and these also became part of the traditional Irish baking repertoire. All the sophisticated modern cooking aids at our disposal today have enabled us to embrace recipes and techniques from all over the world, but there are still some firm traditional favourites, from the simple soda breads that our grandmothers baked, to hearty savoury bakes such as bacon and egg flan (see page 178), with its origins in France, and luscious and sophisticated dessert cakes like chocolate cake made with Guinness (see page 114).

Baking over an open fire with no proper temperature regulation required skill and led to a certain sleight of hand with ingredients – measurements were not rigid and people came to know exactly how many handfuls of flour and cups of buttermilk to throw into the mix. Ovens that can be controlled allow bakers to take full advantage of the subtle chemistry involved in the baking process, as does the wide range of kitchen equipment available today.

Before you embark on your domestic baking career, you should buy a few tins in various shapes and sizes, some wooden spoons, a good rolling pin, a balloon whisk and a wire cooling rack. To achieve good results every time, use a kitchen scales or a measuring jug and spoons; no matter how confident a cook you are, you should always measure your baking ingredients.

If you want to concentrate on bread, you'll need a few loaf tins in various sizes and a baking sheet: you'll need a baking sheet or tray for biscuits, a bun tin for small cakes and muffins, a medium-sized flan tin for tarts and flans and a traybake tin for bars and fingers. When baking large cakes, always use the size and shape specified in the recipe as this really does make the difference between success and failure. You don't need a lot of expensive kit, but if you're going to invest in a single piece of equipment, a good electric stand mixer will make light work of a lot of your baking tasks and will probably last a lifetime.

When you start baking, you may find that simply laying out the ingredients and following a recipe will help you switch off and relax. Once you get the baking bug, your cakes, bread, buns and biscuits will make yours the most popular house in the neighbourhood.

Victorian-era style cooking utensils, Ulster American Folk Park, Omagh

BREAD & SCONES

Tea Room

INGREDIENTS

450 g/1 lb plain white flour, plus extra for dusting

1 tsp salt

1 tsp bicarbonate of soda

400 ml/14 fl oz buttermilk

White Soda Bread

Soda bread is a distinctly Irish bread – unlike yeast bread it does not respond well to too much handling, so don't overwork the dough.

METHOD

Preheat the oven to 230°C/450°F/Gas Mark 8. Dust a baking sheet with flour.

Mix the dry ingredients in a large mixing bowl, then make a well in the centre and gradually add the buttermilk, drawing in the dry ingredients from the sides of the bowl. Mix until a soft dough forms.

Turn out onto a work surface lightly dusted with flour and shape into a round about 5 cm/2 inches in height. Place the round on the prepared baking sheet and use a floured knife to cut a deep cross in it.

Bake in the preheated oven for 30–45 minutes until the loaf sounds hollow when tapped on the base. Transfer to a wire rack and leave to cool completely.

MAKES 1 LOAF

INGREDIENTS

675 g/1 lb 8 oz wholemeal flour

450 g/1 lb strong white flour, plus extra for dusting

2 tsp bicarbonate of soda

2 tsp salt

750 m/1½ pints buttermilk, plus extra if needed

Brown Soda Bread

This is a lovely wholemeal alternative to traditional white soda bread. Wholemeal flour on its own makes a very heavy bread, so white flour is added to the mixture to lighten the texture.

METHOD

Preheat the oven to 230°C/450°F/Gas Mark 8. Dust a large baking sheet with flour.

Mix the dry ingredients in a large mixing bowl, then make a well in the centre and gradually add the buttermilk, drawing in the dry ingredients from the sides of the bowl. Mix until a soft dough forms, adding more buttermilk if necessary. The dough should not be too wet.

Turn out the dough onto a work surface lightly dusted with flour, divide into two pieces and shape both pieces into a round about 5 cm/2 inches in height. Place on the prepared baking sheet and use a floured knife to cut a deep cross in each loaf.

Bake in the preheated oven for 15–20 minutes, then reduce the oven temperature to 200°C/400°F/Gas Mark 6 and bake for a further 20–25 minutes until the loaves sound hollow when tapped on the base. Transfer them to a wire rack and leave to cool completely.

MAKES 2 LOAVES

INGREDIENTS

450 g/1 lb plain
white flour, plus
extra for dusting

1 tsp salt

1 tsp bicarbonate
of soda

125 g/4½ oz
currants, raisins or
sultanas

400 ml/14 fl oz
buttermilk

Currant Bread

Currants or other dried fruit were often
added to white soda bread to make the
traditional 'sweet cake'.

METHOD

Preheat the oven to 230°C/450°F/Gas Mark 8. Dust a baking
sheet with flour.

Mix the dry ingredients in a large mixing bowl, add the currants
and stir until coated in the flour mixture, then make a well in
the centre and gradually add the buttermilk, drawing in the dry
ingredients from the sides of the bowl. Mix to a wet dough.

Turn out the dough onto a work surface lightly dusted with
flour and shape it into a round about 5 cm/2 inches in height.
Place the round on the prepared baking sheet and use a floured
knife to cut a deep cross in it.

Bake in the preheated oven for 30–45 minutes until the loaf
sounds hollow when tapped on the base. Transfer to a wire rack
and leave to cool completely.

MAKES 1 LOAF

INGREDIENTS

vegetable oil, for greasing

1.3 kg/3 lb wholemeal flour

500 ml/18 fl oz milk, plus extra for brushing

500 ml/18 fl oz water

1 tbsp soft light brown sugar

55 g/2 oz fresh yeast

2 tsp salt

Brown Bread

A lovely nutty yeast bread with a slightly sweet flavour. It's well worth taking the time to make it with fresh yeast.

METHOD

Grease two 900-g/2-lb loaf tins and the inside of two large polythene bags.

Put half the flour into a large mixing bowl. Mix the milk and water together in a jug, then add the sugar and yeast. Add to the flour and beat well. Cover the bowl with a damp tea towel and leave to stand for 10–15 minutes, or until the mixture is frothy.

Add the remaining flour and the salt and mix until a soft dough forms. Knead for 10 minutes.

Divide the dough into two pieces and place one piece in each of the prepared tins. Put the tins into the prepared bags and leave to rise until the dough is level with the tops of the tins. Meanwhile, preheat the oven to 230°C/450°F/Gas Mark 8.

Brush the tops of the loaves with milk and bake in the preheated oven for 30–40 minutes until risen and golden brown and they sound hollow when tapped on the base. Transfer to a wire rack and leave to cool completely.

MAKES 2 LOAVES

The Story of Irish Baking

Baking without an oven might seem to be a contradiction in terms, but for the vast majority of the population of Ireland, that's just what home baking involved up to the middle of the 20th century.

In continental Europe, people baked in communal ovens. Fuel was scarce and expensive, so when the baking oven was fired up everyone took advantage of it. In Ireland, fuel was plentiful – every home had a hearth for a turf fire – so cooking could be carried out at home.

A bastible, or pot oven, was used for most forms of cooking in the Irish household. This three- or four-legged cast-iron pot was placed in the hot embers of the fire, and more embers were placed in the concave lid, thus surrounding the entire pot with heat. The even heat produced lent itself to all types of baking and roasting.

The bastible was an ideal vessel for baking traditional soda bread, which became popular in the early 19th century, but it could also be used for baking cakes, meat and fruit pies, scones, cobblers, fadge and even boxty.

The bakestone was introduced at a later stage – rather like a pizza stone, this was preheated over the fire, then used to fry fish and to 'bake' oatcakes and potato cakes. It was easier to control the heat, as the bakestone was suspended over the fire by a chain on a hook and could be raised or lowered depending on the intensity of heat required for the recipe.

19th-century cooking forks and griddle, National Museum of Ireland

The available cooking methods gave rise to a particular emphasis on one-pot cooking. Boiled potatoes, stews, casseroles, pies and soups were all ideal dishes for the bastible oven. Without a hob, there was no way of cooking even a small pot of sauce to serve with meat or fish. Cooking and baking were, therefore, simple and straightforward, with a tendency to rely on plain ingredients that were well cooked without the addition of any fancy herbs and spices. That was for the kitchens of the wealthy.

This type of baking was surprisingly easy and didn't require much labour – as when cooking with a breadmaker or slow cooker, once all the ingredients have been added, the cook can just put the lid on and do something else, raking up the embers occasionally to adjust the heat.

Everything that came out of the bastible, even bread and cakes, was moist. Steam built up inside the vessel, preventing the food drying out. The same principle has been adapted in today's rather more expensive steam ovens.

1946 saw the beginning of the rural electrification scheme in Ireland. Electricity had been available in Dublin since the end of the 19th century, but its widespread introduction throughout the country saw the end of the reliance on the bastible, and people began to use electric ovens. Soon the pot oven was no more than a museum piece and Irish home bakers were able to become ever more inventive with their cooking.

Traditional Irish cooking hearth and utensils

INGREDIENTS

butter, for greasing
900 g/2 lb wholemeal flour
450 g/1 lb strong white flour
55 g/2 oz caster sugar
2 tsp salt
3 sachets easy-blend dried yeast
2 tbsp black treacle
900 ml/1½ pints lukewarm water

Treacle Loaf

This quick bread is great for a baker who is new to yeast – the yeast is simply added with all the other ingredients.

METHOD

Grease a large loaf tin.

Put the wholemeal flour into a bowl and sift in the remaining dry ingredients. Mix the treacle with a little of the water, add to the bowl, then add the remaining water and mix well.

Put the dough into the prepared tin and leave to stand for about 40 minutes, or until doubled in volume. Meanwhile, preheat the oven to 220°C/425°F/Gas Mark 7.

Put the tin into the preheated oven and immediately reduce the oven temperature to 190°C/375°F/Gas Mark 5. Bake for 1 hour, or until the bread is shrinking from the side of the tin and it sounds hollow when tapped on the base.

Leave to cool in the tin for about 5 minutes, then turn out onto a wire rack and leave to cool completely.

MAKES 1 LOAF

INGREDIENTS

butter, for greasing
225 g/8 oz
wholemeal flour
100 g/3½ oz strong
white flour
100 g/3½ oz
oatmeal
1 tsp salt
25 g/1 oz fresh
yeast
600 ml/1 pint
lukewarm water
2 tsp black treacle

Oatmeal Bread

This is a very quick-and-easy yeast bread – no kneading required!

METHOD

Grease a 450-g/1-lb loaf tin. Put the wholemeal flour, white flour, oatmeal and salt into a mixing bowl and stir to combine. Leave to stand in a warm place (an airing cupboard, if you have one).

Put the yeast into a jug with the water and treacle and mix to combine, then leave to stand in a warm place until frothy.

Add the liquid to the dry ingredients and stir until well combined. Transfer the mixture to the prepared tin and leave to stand in a warm place until doubled in volume.

Meanwhile, preheat the oven to 230°C/450°F/Gas Mark 8. Place the tin in the preheated oven and bake for 10 minutes, then reduce the oven temperature to 180°C/350°F/Gas Mark 4 and bake for a further 40 minutes, or until the loaf is shrinking away from the side of the tin and it sounds hollow when tapped on the base.

Leave to cool in the tin for 5 minutes, then turn out onto a wire rack and leave to cool completely.

MAKES 1 LOAF

INGREDIENTS

350 g/12 oz
wholemeal flour

350 g/12 oz plain
white flour, plus
extra for dusting

55 g/2 oz butter,
plus extra for
greasing

2 tbsp sunflower
seeds, plus extra for
sprinkling

2 tbsp sesame seeds

25 g/1 oz soft light
brown sugar

1 tsp salt

1 tsp cream of tartar

1 tsp bicarbonate
of soda

1 tsp baking powder

150 ml/5 fl oz
buttermilk

300 ml/10 fl oz
whole milk

Seed Bread

The seeds add a lovely texture and crunch to this bread – you can experiment with different types of seeds.

METHOD

Preheat the oven to 220°C/425°F/Gas Mark 7. Grease two 450-g/1-lb loaf tins and dust with flour, shaking out any excess.

Put the wholemeal flour and white flour into a bowl, add the butter and rub in until the mixture has the texture of fine breadcrumbs. Add the sunflower seeds, sesame seeds, sugar, salt, cream of tartar, bicarbonate of soda and baking powder and mix well to combine.

Make a well in the centre of the dry mixture and pour in the buttermilk and enough whole milk to mix to a soft dough. Divide the dough into two pieces, knead lightly and place in the prepared tins, pushing it into the corners.

Sprinkle with sunflower seeds and bake in the preheated oven for 40 minutes, or until the loaves sound hollow when tapped on the base. Leave to cool in the tins for 5 minutes, then turn out onto a wire rack and leave to cool completely.

MAKES 2 SMALL LOAVES

INGREDIENTS

butter, for greasing
175 g/6 oz plain
white flour
275 g/9¾ oz
wholemeal flour
1¼ tsp bicarbonate
of soda
3 tsp baking powder
2 tsp salt
1 egg
300 ml/10 fl oz
natural yogurt
150 ml/5 fl oz water
milk, for brushing

Yogurt Soda Bread

This tasty soda bread uses yogurt instead
of buttermilk and is enriched with egg.

METHOD

Preheat the oven to 190°C/375°F/Gas Mark 5. Grease a baking
tray.

Sift the white flour, wholemeal flour, bicarbonate of soda,
baking powder and salt into a bowl, then beat in the egg, yogurt
and water until a soft dough forms.

Shape the dough into a round, place on the prepared baking
tray and cut a cross in the top. Bake in the preheated oven for
35 minutes, then brush the top with milk and bake for a further
10 minutes. Transfer to a wire rack and leave to cool completely.

MAKES 1 LOAF

INGREDIENTS

butter, for greasing

425 g/15 oz strong white flour

3½ tbsp baking powder

55 g/2 oz soft light brown sugar

1 egg, beaten

500 ml/18 fl oz Guinness

Guinness Bread

This unusual bread uses no yeast, relying on the Guinness to help with the rise.

METHOD

Preheat the oven to 200°C/400°F/Gas Mark 6. Grease a 450-g/1-lb loaf tin.

Put the flour, baking powder and sugar into a mixing bowl and stir to combine. Add the egg and Guinness and mix to a wet dough.

Place the dough in the prepared tin, levelling the top. Bake in the preheated oven for 45 minutes, or until the loaf is risen and browned and sounds hollow when tapped on the base.

Leave to cool in the tin for 5 minutes, then turn out onto a wire rack and leave to cool completely.

MAKES 1 LOAF

INGREDIENTS

1.5 kg/3 lb 5 oz raw
potatoes

750 g/1 lb 10 oz
freshly cooked
mashed potatoes

125 g/4½ oz plain
flour

2 tbsp melted
butter, plus extra for
greasing

salt

Oven Boxty Bread

Boxty is a traditional Irish food, made in different ways and named according to the cooking method used. This style of boxty is baked in the oven as a bread.

METHOD

Preheat the oven to 180°C/350°F/Gas Mark 4. Grease a 900-g/2-lb loaf tin.

Grate the raw potatoes and squeeze out as much juice as possible by twisting them in a clean tea towel. Place in a bowl, add the mashed potatoes, flour, butter and a little salt and stir to combine.

Transfer the mixture to the prepared tin, press into the corners, level the top and bake in the preheated oven for 1 hour. Leave to cool in the tin for 5–10 minutes, then turn out onto a plate, slice and serve as a side dish.

SERVES 6-8

INGREDIENTS

225 g/8 oz plain
flour, plus extra for
dusting

pinch of salt

1 heaped tsp baking
powder

55 g/2 oz butter

150 ml/5 fl oz
milk, plus extra for
brushing

Plain White Scones

Scones are a basic recipe and take no time
at all to prepare. Don't overhandle the
dough and get the scones into the oven as
quickly as possible.

METHOD

Preheat the oven to 230°C/450°F/Gas Mark 8. Dust a baking
sheet with flour.

Sift the flour, salt and baking powder into a mixing bowl. Add
the butter and rub it in until fine crumbs form.

Make a well in the centre and add enough milk to mix to a soft
but firm dough. Turn out the dough onto a work surface lightly
dusted with flour and very lightly roll it out to a thickness of 2.5
cm/1 inch. Stamp out 8 rounds, or cut the dough into squares
using a sharp knife.

Place the scones on the prepared baking sheet, brush with a
little milk and bake in the preheated oven for 8–10 minutes
until browned on top and well-risen. Transfer to a wire rack and
leave to cool slightly. Serve warm.

MAKES 8

INGREDIENTS

175 g/6 oz
wholemeal flour,
plus extra for dusting

175 g/6 oz plain
white flour

1 tsp bicarbonate
of soda

½ tsp salt

55 g/2 oz butter

1 tbsp soft light
brown sugar

200 ml/7 fl oz
buttermilk

1 egg, beaten, for
glazing

Wholemeal Scones

These are a great accompaniment to a
hearty winter soup, or could be served
with butter and home-made jam.

METHOD

Preheat the oven to 200°C/400°F/Gas Mark 6. Dust a baking
sheet with flour.

Put the wholemeal flour, white flour, salt and bicarbonate of
soda into a bowl and mix to combine. Add the butter and rub
it in with your fingertips until fine crumbs form. Add the sugar
and mix to combine.

Add enough buttermilk to mix to a soft dough. Turn out the
dough onto a work surface lightly dusted with flour and knead
for a few seconds.

Press out the dough to a thickness of 4 cm/1½ inches, then use
a 6-cm/2½-inch round biscuit cutter to cut out 8–10 rounds,
reshaping the trimmings as necessary.

Place the scones on the prepared baking sheet, then brush with
the beaten egg and bake in the preheated oven for 15 minutes,
or until risen and golden. Transfer to a wire rack and leave to
cool slightly. Serve warm.

MAKES 8-10

INGREDIENTS

450 g/1 lb self-raising flour, plus extra for dusting

pinch of salt

100 g/3½ oz chilled butter, diced

85 g/3 oz caster sugar

300 m/10 fl oz buttermilk

whole milk, for brushing

Buttermilk Scones

These lovely scones are perfect for serving at afternoon tea, with lashings of butter and home-made jam.

METHOD

Preheat the oven to 220°C/425°F/Gas Mark 7. Dust a baking sheet with flour.

Put the flour and salt into a bowl. Add the butter and rub it in with your fingertips until fine crumbs form. Add the sugar and mix to combine.

Heat the buttermilk over a low heat until lukewarm. Gradually add to the flour mixture, cutting it in with a knife until just combined.

Turn out the dough onto a work surface lightly dusted with flour and bring it together with your hands. Press it out to a thickness of 4 cm/1½ inches, then use a 6-cm/2½-inch round biscuit cutter to cut out 12 rounds, reshaping the trimmings as necessary.

Place the scones on the prepared baking sheet, then brush with a little milk and bake in the preheated oven for 10–12 minutes until golden. Remove from the oven, transfer to a wire rack and leave to cool slightly. Serve warm.

MAKES 12

Cheddar Cheese Scones

These make a good lunchtime scone, and are delicious served with soup. Use a really mature Cheddar for the best flavour.

INGREDIENTS

225 g/8 oz plain white flour, plus extra for dusting

1 heaped tsp baking powder

55 g/2 oz butter, plus extra for greasing

100 g/3½ oz extra-mature Cheddar cheese, grated

1 tsp English mustard powder

100 ml/3½ fl oz milk, plus extra for brushing

salt and freshly ground black pepper

METHOD

Preheat the oven to 230°C/450°F/Gas Mark 8. Grease a large baking sheet.

Sift the flour and baking powder into a mixing bowl, then cut in the butter and rub it in with your fingertips until fine crumbs form. Mix in the cheese and mustard, adding salt and pepper to taste.

Make a well in the centre of the dry ingredients and add the milk, mixing to a soft dough. Turn out the dough onto a work surface lightly dusted with flour and roll out to a thickness of 2 cm/¾ inch.

Using a lightly floured fluted round cutter, cut out 10 scones and place them on the prepared baking sheet. Brush with milk and bake in the preheated oven for 10–15 minutes, or until well-risen and golden. Transfer to a wire rack and leave to cool. Eat on the day of baking.

MAKES 10

INGREDIENTS

butter, for greasing
175 g/6 oz
wholemeal flour,
plus extra for dusting
55 g/2 oz porridge
oats, plus extra for
sprinkling
1 heaped tsp
bicarbonate of soda
large pinch of salt
55 g/2 oz white
vegetable fat
150 ml/5 fl oz
buttermilk
beaten egg, for
brushing

Oat Scones

A great breakfast scone, made with
standard porridge oats.

METHOD

Preheat the oven to 230°C/450°F/Gas Mark 8. Grease a baking
sheet.

Put the flour, oats, bicarbonate of soda, salt and vegetable fat
into a mixing bowl and mix well to combine. Make a well in the
centre and add enough buttermilk to mix to a fairly soft dough.

Turn out the dough onto a work surface lightly dusted with
flour, knead lightly, then roll out to a thickness of 2 cm/¾ inch.
Using a sharp knife, cut the dough into 8 squares.

Place the squares on the prepared baking sheet, brush with
beaten egg and sprinkle with oats. Bake in the preheated oven
for 8–10 minutes until risen and browned. Transfer to a wire
rack and leave to cool. Eat the scones on the day of baking.

MAKES 8

INGREDIENTS

100 g/3½ oz plain
flour, plus extra for
dusting

1 tsp baking powder

large pinch of salt

55 g/2 oz butter,
plus extra for
greasing

4 tbsp mashed
potatoes

milk, for mixing and
brushing

butter, to serve

Potato Scones

Just a small amount of leftover mashed potatoes gives these scones a light texture and hearty flavour.

METHOD

Preheat the oven to 180°C/350°F/Gas Mark 4. Grease a baking sheet.

Sift the flour, baking powder and salt together into a bowl, then rub in the butter. Add the potatoes and a little milk and mix to a soft dough.

Turn out the dough onto a work surface lightly dusted with flour and roll out to a thickness of 2 cm/¾ inch. Use a floured cutter to cut out rounds, then place them on the prepared baking sheet.

Brush the tops with milk and bake in the preheated oven for about 15 minutes until golden brown. Transfer to a wire rack and leave to cool slightly. Serve warm with butter.

MAKES ABOUT 6

Baking with Buttermilk

Buttermilk is used to add lightness and softness to breads, scones and cakes. When combined with bicarbonate of soda or baking powder the buttermilk begins to fizz, and this chemical reaction also cancels out the sour taste of the buttermilk.

Buttermilk is an essential ingredient in soda bread. It lends itself particularly well to the soft wheat flour traditionally used in Ireland, which didn't have the structure to support the use of yeast as a raising agent.

Buttermilk itself is a by-product of butter churning – it's the thin liquid left behind. Many families had a milk cow and the butter they made was sold to provide a small income. When butter making became a commercial concern, dairies sold off the buttermilk cheaply at the end of the day, profiting from selling what would otherwise be discarded. People no longer queue outside dairies for the leavings of the butter churning – commercial buttermilk is produced by adding a bacterial culture to skimmed milk.

IF YOU CAN'T GET BUTTERMILK, THERE ARE SEVERAL EASY SUBSTITUTES:

Natural yogurt – make up a 3:1 mixture of yogurt and water.

Soured cream – make up a 3:1 mixture of soured cream and water.

Kefir – thin the kefir with water or milk until it has the consistency of buttermilk.

You can also use cream of tartar to make buttermilk. Mix 225 ml/8 fl oz whole milk with 1¾ teaspoons cream of tartar. Stir and leave to stand for 5–10 minutes until thick and curdled.

Use a liquid acid such as lemon juice or vinegar for a handy buttermilk substitute made with everyday storecupboard ingredients – mix 225 ml/8 fl oz whole milk or cream with 1 tablespoon of lemon juice or white vinegar. Leave to stand for 5–10 minutes until slightly curdled.

The chemistry that enables buttermilk to be used in baking was identified in France in 1791. Alkaline bicarbonate of soda produced a 'raising' action when combined with the acid in buttermilk. Bicarbonate of soda was inexpensive, so bread could be produced easily and cheaply with limited cooking facilities. Yeast bread needs a temperature-regulated oven, and most Irish homes were limited to using a cast-iron pot over the fire.

The simple ingredients for soda bread – flour, buttermilk, bicarbonate of soda and salt – are mixed together quickly (no need for proving) to make a simple and wholesome bread, as delicious as any yeast bread, and now celebrated worldwide. It can be savoury or sweet, white or wholemeal, and dried fruit was sometimes added as a sweetener for special occasions – perhaps this is why soda bread is always referred to as a 'cake' rather than a 'loaf'?

THE CROSS IN THE TOP OF THE SODA BREAD

Traditionally, a deep cross is cut in the top of the cake of soda bread before baking, giving it its distinctive appearance. Mothers used to tell their children that the cross allowed the fairies to escape. Others believed that it 'let the devil out' of the bread. The purpose of the cross is actually to allow the steam to escape during baking, producing a lighter-textured bread.

Cinnamon Fruit Scones

INGREDIENTS

450 g/1 lb plain flour, plus extra for dusting

175 g/6 oz butter

1 heaped tsp baking powder

85 g/3 oz sugar

1 tsp cinnamon

100 g/3½ oz mixed currants, raisins and sultanas

2 eggs, beaten

milk, for mixing and brushing

These traditional fruit scones are given a little added spice with the addition of cinnamon. You could ring the changes with chopped dried dates or figs.

METHOD

Preheat the oven to 180°C/350°F/Gas Mark 4. Dust a baking sheet with flour.

Sift the flour into a mixing bowl. Cut in the butter and rub it in with your fingertips until fine crumbs form. Add the baking powder and mix well to combine. Add the sugar, cinnamon and dried fruit and stir.

Make a well in the centre and add the eggs and enough milk to mix to a soft dough. Turn out the dough onto a work surface lightly dusted with flour and roll it out very lightly to a thickness of 2.5 cm/1 inch. Stamp out 16 rounds, or cut the dough into squares using a sharp knife.

Place the scones on the prepared baking sheet, brush with a little milk and bake in the preheated oven for 25–35 minutes until well risen and golden. Transfer to a wire rack and leave to cool slightly. Serve warm.

MAKES 16

INGREDIENTS

butter, for greasing

225 g/8 oz quick-cook polenta

225 g/8 oz plain white flour, plus extra for dusting

½ tsp bicarbonate of soda

½ tsp cream of tartar

½ tsp salt

1 tbsp sugar

55 g/2 oz lard or vegetable shortening

buttermilk, for mixing

Cornmeal Scones

These were originally made with cornmeal, which was readily available but had to be soaked before using. Using quick-cook polenta reduces the preparation time significantly.

METHOD

Preheat the oven to 200°C/400°F/Gas Mark 6. Grease a large baking sheet.

Put the polenta into a mixing bowl and sift in the flour, bicarbonate of soda, cream of tartar, salt and sugar. Rub in the lard, then add enough buttermilk to mix to a soft dough.

Turn out the dough onto a work surface lightly dusted with flour and roll out to a thickness of 2 cm/¾ inch. Cut into 16 squares, place on the prepared baking sheet and bake in the preheated oven for 15–20 minutes. Transfer to a wire rack and leave to cool slightly. Serve warm or cold.

MAKES 16

INGREDIENTS

250 g/9 oz plain
flour, plus extra for
dusting
1 tsp baking powder
½ tsp salt
55 g/2 oz butter,
plus extra for
greasing
55 g/2 oz rolled oats
85 g/3 oz caster
sugar
6-7 tbsp milk

Topping

2 tbsp golden syrup
15 g/½ oz butter
25 g/1 oz rolled oats

Oat & Syrup Scones

A textured sweet scone with a luscious syrupy crunch topping.

METHOD

Preheat the oven to 220°C/425°F/Gas Mark 7. Grease a baking sheet.

Sift the flour, baking powder and salt into a bowl. Rub in the butter with your fingertips until the mixture resembles breadcrumbs. Add the oats, sugar and milk and stir until a soft dough forms.

Knead the dough briefly, then turn it out onto a work surface lightly dusted with flour and roll out to a thickness of 3 cm/1¼ inches. Use a floured cutter to cut out rounds, then place them on the prepared baking sheet.

To make the topping, heat the golden syrup and butter together in a small saucepan until the butter is melted, then remove from the heat and add the oats. Spoon some of the mixture onto each scone, then bake in the preheated oven for 12–15 minutes. Transfer to a wire rack and leave to cool slightly.

MAKES ABOUT 12

INGREDIENTS

450 g/1 lb plain
flour, plus extra for
dusting

large pinch of salt

1 tsp baking powder

175 g/6 oz butter,
plus extra for
greasing

55 g/2 oz caster
sugar

300 ml/10 fl oz
buttermilk

Butter Cakes

These are very popular in the northern
counties of Ireland. They get their name
from the generous quantity of butter used.

METHOD

Preheat the oven to 220°C/425°F/Gas Mark 7. Grease a large
baking sheet.

Sift the flour, salt and baking powder into a mixing bowl. Cut
in the butter and rub it in with your fingertips until fine crumbs
form. Add the sugar and mix well. Add enough buttermilk to
mix to a soft but not wet dough.

Turn out onto a work surface lightly dusted with flour and
knead very lightly. Roll out to a thickness of 2 cm/¾ inch and
cut into 16 rounds.

Place the rounds on the prepared baking sheet and bake in the
preheated oven for 15–20 minutes until well risen and golden.
Transfer to a wire rack and leave to cool slightly. Serve warm
with butter and jam.

MAKES 16

INGREDIENTS

225 g/8 oz self-raising flour, plus extra for dusting

½ tsp baking powder

large pinch of salt

55 g/2 oz butter, plus extra for greasing

175 g/6 oz mashed potatoes

buttermilk, for mixing

Oven-baked Fadge

Potato cakes are traditionally 'baked' on a griddle, but this oven method is just as good. You can use leftover mashed potatoes if you like, but these will taste better if the potatoes are freshly cooked.

METHOD

Preheat the oven to 220°C/425°F/Gas Mark 7. Grease a large baking tray.

Sift the flour into a mixing bowl with the baking powder and salt and rub in the butter. Add the potatoes and mix well to combine.

Add enough buttermilk to mix to a soft dough, then turn out onto a work surface lightly dusted with flour and knead lightly. Roll out the dough to a thickness of 2 cm/¾ inch and cut into 12 squares with a sharp knife.

Place the squares on the prepared tray and bake in the preheated oven for 20–25 minutes until risen, golden and crisp. Serve hot.

MAKES 12

INGREDIENTS

225 g/8 oz butter, plus extra for greasing

225 g/8 oz soft light brown sugar

300 ml/10 fl oz Irish stout

225 g/8 oz raisins

225 g/8 oz sultanas

115 g/4 oz chopped mixed peel

450 g/1 lb plain flour

½ tsp bicarbonate of soda

½ tsp allspice

½ tsp ground nutmeg

115 g/4 oz glacé cherries, halved

finely grated rind of 1 lemon

3 eggs, beaten

Porter Cake

A rich fruit cake, steeped in stout for extra depth of flavour.

METHOD

Preheat the oven to 180°C/350°F/Gas Mark 4. Grease a 25-cm/10-inch round cake tin and line with baking paper.

Put the butter, sugar and stout into a saucepan and heat over a low heat until the butter is melted. Add the raisins, sultanas and mixed peel, bring to the boil, then simmer for 10 minutes.

Leave to cool, then add the flour, bicarbonate of soda, allspice, nutmeg, cherries and lemon rind. Gradually add the eggs and mix well to combine.

Pour the batter into the prepared tin and bake in the preheated oven for about 1½ hours, or until a skewer inserted into the centre comes out clean. Leave to cool in the tin, then turn out onto a plate. This cake can be stored in an airtight tin for up to 1 week.

SERVES 12

INGREDIENTS

85 g/3 oz butter, plus extra for greasing

150 g/5½ oz caster sugar

2 eggs, beaten

4 very ripe bananas, mashed well

225 g/8 oz self-raising flour

1 tsp mixed spice

1 tsp salt

100 g/3½ oz chopped walnuts

Banana & Walnut Loaf

Make this nutty loaf with very ripe bananas for delicious sweetness and texture.

METHOD

Preheat the oven to 180°C/350°F/Gas Mark 4. Grease a 900-g/2-lb loaf tin.

Put the butter into a bowl and cream until soft, then add the eggs and sugar and beat until smooth.

Add the bananas and stir to combine. Sift in the flour, mixed spice and salt and mix well. Add the walnuts and stir until evenly distributed.

Pour the batter into the prepared tin and bake in the preheated oven for 1 hour–1 hour 10 minutes until golden brown. Cover with a piece of foil if the top is browning too quickly. Leave to cool in the tin for 10 minutes, then turn out onto a wire rack and leave to cool completely.

MAKES 1 LOAF

INGREDIENTS

150 g/5½ oz caster sugar

150 g/5½ oz butter, plus extra for greasing

3 eggs, lightly beaten

150 g/5½ oz self-raising flour

1½ tsp baking powder

½ tsp vanilla extract

icing sugar, for dusting

Filling

4 tbsp raspberry jam

250 ml/9 fl oz double cream, whipped

Victoria Sponge

This traditional afternoon tea sponge is even more delicious when home-made jam is used for the filling.

METHOD

Preheat the oven to 160°C/325°F/Gas Mark 3. Grease two 20-cm/8-inch sandwich tins and line the bases with baking paper.

Put the butter and sugar into a bowl and cream together until pale and fluffy. Gradually add the eggs, alternating with two-thirds of the flour. Fold in the baking powder with the remaining flour and the vanilla extract.

Divide the batter between the prepared tins and bake in the preheated oven for 30 minutes. Leave to cool in the tins for 10 minutes, then turn out onto a wire rack and leave to cool completely.

For the filling, spread the jam on the base of one of the cakes. Spread the cream on the jam and place the other cake on top to make a sandwich. Dust with icing sugar and serve.

SERVES 8

INGREDIENTS

175 g/6 oz butter, softened, plus extra for greasing

175 g/6 oz caster sugar

175 g/6 oz self-raising flour, sifted

4 eggs, beaten

finely grated zest of 3 lemons

3 tsp lemon extract

icing sugar, for dusting

Lemon Cake

This tangy lemon cake is delicious served with coffee or tea, or with whipped cream or ice cream as a dessert.

METHOD

Preheat the oven to 180°C/350°F/Gas Mark 4. Grease a 23-cm/9-inch round springform cake tin and line with baking paper.

Cream the butter and sugar together until pale and fluffy. Gradually add the flour and the eggs alternately, beating after each addition until incorporated.

Add the lemon zest and lemon extract, stirring well to combine. The batter will be quite stiff.

Transfer the batter to the prepared tin and bake in the preheated oven for 20 minutes. Reduce the oven temperature to 160°C/300°F/Gas Mark 2 and bake for a further 20–30 minutes until a skewer inserted into the centre of the cake comes out clean.

Leave to cool in the tin for 10 minutes, then unclip and remove the springform and leave to cool completely. Transfer to a plate, dust with icing sugar and serve.

SERVES 8

INGREDIENTS

240 g/8½ oz butter, softened, plus extra for greasing

240 g/8½ oz caster sugar

4 large eggs, beaten

25 g/1 oz caraway seeds

½ tsp ground mace

½ tsp freshly ground nutmeg

325 g/11½ oz self-raising flour

3 tbsp brandy

4-6 tbsp milk

soft light brown sugar, for sprinkling

Seed Cake

This classic cake has a surprisingly sophisticated flavour. Don't be too heavy-handed with the caraway seeds!

METHOD

Preheat the oven to 180°C/350°F/Gas Mark 4. Grease an 18-cm/7-inch round cake tin and line the base with baking paper.

Cream the butter and caster sugar together in a large bowl until pale and fluffy, then gradually add the eggs, beating after each addition until incorporated.

Add the caraway seeds, mace and nutmeg, then sift in the flour and fold it in. Stir in the brandy.

Add enough milk to loosen the batter to a good dropping consistency. Spoon the batter into the prepared tin, smoothing the surface with the back of a spoon. Sprinkle with brown sugar and bake in the middle of the preheated oven for 40–50 minutes, or until a skewer inserted into the centre of the cake comes out clean.

Leave to cool in the tin for 10 minutes, then turn out onto a wire rack and leave to cool completely.

SERVES 6-8

INGREDIENTS

500 g/1 lb 2 oz
Bramley apples,
peeled, cored and
cut into chunks

2 tbsp soft light
brown sugar

250 g/9 oz plain
flour, plus extra if
needed

½ tsp baking powder

100 g/3½ oz chilled
butter, plus extra for
greasing

100 g/3½ oz caster
sugar

1 large egg, beaten

100 ml/3½ fl oz
milk

Kerry Apple Cake

This cake is a cross between an apple tart and an apple pie. The texture of the pastry – a bit like a soft shortbread – is key.

METHOD

Preheat the oven to 180°C/350°F/Gas Mark 4. Grease a 20-cm/8-inch round loose-based cake tin and line the base with baking paper.

Toss the apples with the brown sugar. Sift the flour and baking powder together into a bowl and rub in the butter with your fingertips until fine crumbs form.

Add the caster sugar, mixing it in with a blunt knife, then add the egg. Add the milk very gradually and mix until a soft dough forms. Add a little more flour if the mixture becomes too wet to handle.

Spread half the dough in the base of the prepared tin. Tip in the apples, then spread the remaining dough on top. Bake in the preheated oven for 40 minutes, or until the dough is golden and the apples are tender. Leave to cool in the tin for about 10 minutes, then turn out and serve.

SERVES 8

Ginger Cake

INGREDIENTS

175 g/6 oz black treacle

55 g/2 oz golden syrup

100 g/3½ oz butter, plus extra for greasing

150 ml/5 fl oz milk

2 eggs, beaten

225 g/8 oz plain flour

55 g/2 oz caster sugar

2 tsp mixed spice

2 tsp ground ginger

1 tsp bicarbonate of soda

This is a traditional cut-and-come-again cake. The treacle and golden syrup keep it moist and the mixed spice and ginger add a warm depth of flavour.

METHOD

Preheat the oven to 150°C/300°F/Gas Mark 2. Grease a 450-g/1-lb loaf tin and line it with baking paper.

Put the treacle, golden syrup and butter into a saucepan and heat over a medium heat until the butter is melted. Add the milk and the eggs.

Sift the flour, sugar, mixed spice, ginger and bicarbonate of soda together into a bowl. Add the treacle mixture and beat until smooth.

Pour the batter into the prepared tin and bake in the preheated oven for 1¼–1½ hours, or until a skewer inserted into the centre of the cake comes out clean.

Leave to cool in the tin for 10 minutes, then turn out onto a wire rack and leave to cool completely. Slice and serve.

SERVES 6–8

INGREDIENTS

340 g/11¾ oz plain flour, plus extra for dusting

½ tsp bicarbonate of soda

pinch of salt

55 g/2 oz caster sugar, plus extra for sprinkling

85 g/3 oz butter, plus extra for greasing

1 egg

175 ml/6 fl oz buttermilk

700 g/1 lb 9 oz rhubarb, trimmed and cut into chunks

200 g/7 oz demerara sugar

milk, for brushing

whipped cream, to serve

SERVES 6-8

Rhubarb Cake

This is a cross between a pie and a cake. The 'pastry' is a scone dough, and the thick syrup from the fruit soaks into it while cooking, making a very moist cake.

METHOD

Preheat the oven to 180°C/350°F/Gas Mark 4. Grease a 25-cm/10-inch pie dish.

Sift the flour, bicarbonate of soda and salt into a large bowl. Add the caster sugar and rub in the butter until fine crumbs form.

Put the egg into a separate bowl, add the buttermilk and beat well, then gradually add to the flour mixture, mixing to a firm but soft dough.

Turn out the dough onto a work surface lightly dusted with flour, knead lightly, divide into two pieces and roll out both pieces. Use one piece to line the prepared dish.

Add the rhubarb to the dish, sprinkle over the demerara sugar, then brush the rim of the base with a little water and cover with the second piece of dough. Crimp the edges together, brush with milk and sprinkle over some caster sugar. Pierce with a fork several times.

Bake in the preheated oven for 50–55 minutes, or until the top is golden. Leave to cool for 10–15 minutes, then serve warm with whipped cream.

INGREDIENTS

225 ml/8 fl oz cold tea

200 g/7 oz sugar

175 g/6 oz mixed sultanas and raisins

1 tsp mixed spice

1 tsp ground cinnamon

25 g/1 oz butter, plus extra for greasing and serving

250 g/9 oz self-raising flour

1 egg, beaten

Irish Tea Cake

The unusual flavour and texture of this popular cake is produced by soaking the dried fruit in tea.

METHOD

Put the tea, sugar, dried fruit, mixed spice, cinnamon and butter into a saucepan and bring to the boil over a low heat, stirring constantly. Remove from the heat and leave to cool.

Meanwhile, preheat the oven to 180°C/350°F/Gas Mark 4. Grease a 900-g/2-lb loaf tin and line the base and sides with baking paper.

Add the flour and the egg to the cooled mixture and beat until well combined.

Pour the batter into the prepared tin and bake in the preheated oven for about 1 hour, or until a skewer inserted into the centre of the cake comes out clean. Cover with foil if the top is browning too quickly.

Leave to cool in the tin for 10 minutes, then turn out onto a wire rack and leave to cool completely. Peel off the baking paper, slice thickly and serve with butter.

SERVES 8

INGREDIENTS

225 g/8 oz sultanas
grated zest of 1
lemon
150 ml/5 fl oz Irish
whiskey
175 g/6 oz butter,
softened, plus extra
for greasing
175 g/6 oz soft light
brown sugar
175 g/6 oz self-
raising flour
pinch of salt
pinch of ground
nutmeg
4 eggs, separated

Whiskey Cake

The sultanas absorb the whiskey really well, so this cake is very moist and full of warm whiskey flavour.

METHOD

Put the sultanas in a bowl with the lemon zest and pour over the whiskey. Cover and leave to soak overnight.

Preheat the oven to 180°C/350°F/Gas Mark 4. Grease an 18-cm/7-inch round loose-based cake tin and line with baking paper.

Put the butter and sugar into a bowl and cream until pale and fluffy. Sift the flour, salt and nutmeg into a separate bowl. Beat the egg yolks and gradually add to the butter and sugar mixture with a little of the flour mixture, beating well after each addition.

Gradually add the sultana and whiskey mixture, alternating with the remaining flour mixture, stirring lightly to combine.

Whisk the egg whites until they hold stiff peaks, then fold into the mixture with a metal spoon. Do not over-mix.

Transfer the batter to the prepared tin and bake in the preheated oven for 1½ hours, until the cake is well risen and a skewer inserted into the centre comes out clean. Leave to cool in the tin for 10 minutes, then turn out onto a wire rack and leave to cool completely.

SERVES 8

INGREDIENTS

225 g/8 oz self-
raising flour
pinch of salt
pinch of mixed spice
100 g/3½ oz butter
100 g/3½ oz
demerara sugar, plus
extra for sprinkling
100 g/3½ oz dried
stoned dates,
roughly chopped
1 egg, beaten
4 tbsp milk

Date Loaf

This is lovely served warm, with butter. It's best eaten on the day of baking, but any leftovers are delicious toasted.

METHOD

Preheat the oven to 180°C/350°F/Gas Mark 4. Grease a 450-g/1-lb loaf tin with butter and line with baking paper.

Sift the flour, salt and mixed spice into a mixing bowl. Add the butter and rub it in with your fingertips until fine crumbs form.

Stir in the sugar and dates, then add the egg and milk and mix well to combine – the batter should have a good dropping consistency. Transfer the batter to the prepared tin, levelling the top. Sprinkle with a little sugar and bake in the preheated oven for 1½ hours until golden and a skewer inserted into the centre of the cake comes out clean.

Leave to cool in the tin for 10 minutes, then turn out onto a wire rack and leave to cool completely.

SERVES 8

Baking with Potatoes

Potatoes, the staple diet of the Irish for centuries, have uses that extend far beyond simple boiling, baking and frying. Mixing cooked potatoes with flour produces delicious bread and cakes with an unexpectedly moist texture.

Boxty is usually made with grated raw potatoes and a little flour, shaped into a flat cake and fried in a pan, but a variation of the traditional recipe is a combination of raw and cooked potatoes, baked in the oven (see page 36).

The simple savoury potato cake, traditionally fried in a pan or on a griddle (but just as good baked), is a great way to use up leftover mashed potatoes and is still a popular Sunday evening snack after the filling Sunday roast. To keep them as light as possible, use about 75 per cent mashed potatoes to 25 per cent plain flour, mix well with salt, black pepper, chives and a little melted butter and shape into patties. Bake on a lined baking sheet in a hot oven for 10 minutes. You can bring them right up to date by sprinkling them with a little Parmesan cheese before putting them in the oven.

Beyond savoury baking, potatoes have been an unexpectedly useful ingredient in Irish sweet baking. Apple potato cake is a type of farl made with mashed potatoes, apples and a little flour. It's usually cooked on the griddle, but a different version, using the same combination of ingredients, is a delicious apple pie made with a potato pastry – the moist pastry is wonderfully crisp on the outside. Spiced potato cake, made with raisins (see page 90), made a frequent appearance on the tea table, and potatoes are now being used in ingenious and unlikely ways – they are even combined with chocolate to make deliciously light, moist cakes (see page 92).

Using potatoes for baking is nothing new, but for those with wheat or gluten sensitivities this uninspiring white tuber has almost magical properties. Potato starch flour is, as its name suggests, a flour made from potato starch. It is an excellent substitute for wheat flour and gives a light and airy result to all baked goods. It shouldn't, however, be confused with the stodgier potato flour, which should be used sparingly and always in conjunction with wheat flour.

INGREDIENTS

250 g/9 oz self-raising flour, plus extra for dusting

pinch of salt

6 tsp mixed spice

150 g/5½ oz butter, softened, plus extra for greasing

400 g/14 oz caster sugar

2 eggs, beaten

175 ml/6 fl oz milk

425 g/15 oz mashed potatoes

150 g/5 oz raisins or sultanas

Spiced Potato Cake

The main ingredient in this delicious cake is potatoes. It is best prepared with freshly cooked mashed potatoes rather than leftovers.

METHOD

Preheat the oven to 160°C/325°F/Gas Mark 3. Grease a 25-cm/10-inch round cake tin and dust with flour, shaking out any excess.

Sift the flour, salt and mixed spice into a bowl. Put the butter and sugar into a separate bowl and cream together until pale and fluffy. Beat in the eggs, then gradually add the flour mixture, alternating with the milk and potatoes.

Stir in the raisins, then pour the batter into the prepared tin and bake in the preheated oven for 1½–2 hours, or until a skewer inserted into the centre of the cake comes out clean. Leave to cool in the tin for 10 minutes, then turn out onto a wire rack and leave to cool completely.

SERVES 8-10

INGREDIENTS

175 g/6 oz butter, softened

175 g/6 oz caster sugar

2 eggs, beaten

150 g/5 oz self-raising flour

25 g/1 oz cocoa power

1 heaped tsp baking powder

55 g/2 oz mashed potatoes

3 tbsp milk

icing sugar, for dusting

Chocolate Potato Cake

This delicious cake relies on potatoes for its light texture.

METHOD

Preheat the oven to 190°C/350°F/Gas Mark 5. Grease a 25-cm/10-inch round cake tin and line with baking paper.

Put the butter and caster sugar into a mixing bowl and cream until pale and fluffy. Gradually add the beaten egg, beating well after each addition.

Sift in the flour, cocoa powder and baking powder and fold in lightly with a metal spoon. Add the mashed potatoes and milk and stir to combine.

Pour the batter into the prepared tin and bake in the preheated oven for 35–40 minutes, or until a skewer inserted into the centre comes out clean.

Leave to cool in the tin for 10 minutes, then turn out onto a wire rack and leave to cool completely. Dust with icing sugar just before serving.

SERVES 8-10

INGREDIENTS

100 g/3½ oz butter, softened, plus extra for greasing

100 g/3½ oz caster sugar

2 tsp clear honey

150 g/5½ oz self-raising flour, plus extra for dusting

½ tsp baking powder

2 tbsp milk

2 eggs

3 tbsp Irish Mist liqueur

Glaze

175 g/6 oz plain chocolate, broken into pieces

300 ml/10 fl oz water

100 g/3½ oz granulated sugar

Irish Mist Ring Cake

This is very simple to make but looks impressive – it's a bit sticky, so it's best eaten with a fork!

METHOD

Preheat the oven to 190°C/375°F/Gas Mark 5. Grease a 20-cm/8-inch ring tin and dust with flour, shaking out any excess.

Put all the cake ingredients, except the liqueur, into a mixing bowl and beat well until smooth. Add 1 tablespoon of the liqueur and beat to combine. Pour the batter into the prepared tin and bake in the preheated oven for 35–40 minutes.

Leave to cool in the tin for 10 minutes, then turn out onto a serving plate and slowly pour over the remaining liqueur. Leave to cool completely before glazing.

To make the glaze, put the chocolate into a saucepan with the water and heat gently, stirring until melted. Add the sugar and simmer, uncovered, for 15 minutes until thick and shiny.

Pour the glaze over the cake, allowing it to dribble down the sides. Leave to cool and set before serving.

SERVES 6–8

INGREDIENTS

225 g/8 oz self-raising flour

pinch of salt

225 g/8 oz glacé cherries, quartered, plus a few whole cherries to decorate

175 g/6 oz butter, plus extra for greasing

175 g/6 oz caster sugar

3 eggs, beaten

4 tbsp milk

¼ tsp vanilla extract

demerara sugar, for sprinkling

Cherry Cake

Glacé cherries are a great storecupboard standby, and they add an old-fashioned touch to an afternoon tea cake.

METHOD

Preheat the oven to 180°C/350°F/Gas Mark 4. Grease a 20-cm/8-inch round loose-based cake tin and line with baking paper.

Sift the flour and salt into a mixing bowl. Add the quartered cherries and mix until coated with the flour.

Put the butter and caster sugar into a separate bowl and cream together until light and fluffy. Beat in the eggs, one at a time, adding a little of the flour with each addition. Mix well, then stir in the flour, milk and vanilla extract and mix until quite stiff.

Put the batter into the prepared tin and level the top. Halve some whole glacé cherries and press them into the top of the cake. Sprinkle with demerara sugar and bake in the preheated oven for 1½ hours until golden and a skewer inserted into the centre of the cake comes out clean.

Leave to cool in the tin for 10–15 minutes, then turn out onto a wire rack and leave to cool completely before peeling off the baking paper.

SERVES 6-8

INGREDIENTS

150 g/5½ oz caster sugar

150 g/5½ oz butter, plus extra for greasing

3 eggs, lightly beaten

150 g/5½ oz self-raising flour

1½ tsp baking powder

4 tbsp coffee essence or cold espresso coffee

walnut halves, to decorate

Butter cream

100 g/3½ oz butter

225 g/8 oz icing sugar

2 tbsp coffee essence or cold espresso coffee

SERVES 8

Coffee & Walnut Cake

Before coffee became a popular drink in Ireland, most storecupboards contained a bottle of concentrated coffee essence for use in baking.

METHOD

Preheat the oven to 160°C/325°F/Gas Mark 3. Grease two 20-cm/8-inch sandwich tins and line the bases with baking paper.

Beat the sugar and butter together until light and fluffy. Gradually add the eggs, alternating with two-thirds of the flour. Fold in the baking powder with the remaining flour. Add the coffee essence and fold in carefully.

Divide the batter between the prepared tins and bake in the preheated oven for 30 minutes. Leave to cool in the tins for 10 minutes, then turn out onto a wire rack and leave to cool completely.

Meanwhile, to make the butter cream, cream the butter and sugar until light and fluffy. Gradually add the coffee essence, mixing after each addition until incorporated. Chill in the refrigerator until needed.

Spread half the butter cream on the base of one of the cakes and top with the other cake. Spread the remaining icing on top, decorate with walnut halves and serve.

INGREDIENTS

175 g/6 oz plain chocolate

6 eggs, separated

175 g/6 oz caster sugar, plus extra for sprinkling

1 tbsp cocoa powder, sifted

Filling

300 ml/10 fl oz double cream

2 tbsp icing sugar

a mixture of icing sugar and cocoa powder, to decorate

Chocolate Swiss Roll

Swiss roll has always been a popular choice – this light and airy flourless version is simply delicious.

METHOD

Preheat the oven to 180°C/350°F/Gas Mark 4. Grease a 23 x 33-cm/ 9 x 13-inch Swiss roll tin and line with baking paper. Put the chocolate in a heatproof bowl set over a saucepan of gently simmering water and heat until melted.

Put the egg whites into a large grease-free bowl and whisk until they hold soft peaks. Set aside until needed. Put the egg yolks and caster sugar into a large heatproof bowl set over a saucepan of gently simmering water. Whisk until the mixture is thick enough to leave a trail when the whisk is lifted. Stir in the chocolate, then gently fold in the egg whites. Fold in the cocoa powder. Pour the batter into the prepared tin and bake in the preheated oven for 20–25 minutes, or until the centre of the cake springs back when lightly touched with your finger.

Meanwhile, lay a sheet of baking paper on the work surface and sprinkle with a little caster sugar. Turn out the sponge onto the paper, then carefully peel away the lining paper. Trim the edges and cover the sponge with a damp tea towel. Leave to cool.

To make the filling, whip the cream with the icing sugar until it holds soft peaks, then spread it over the sponge. Starting from one of the narrow ends, carefully roll up the sponge using the paper to help – don't worry if it cracks a little. Transfer to a serving plate, dust with a mixture of icing sugar and cocoa powder and serve.

SERVES 12

INGREDIENTS

225 g/8 oz ready-made shortcrust pastry

300 g/10½ oz stale cake or bread

75 g/2¾ oz plain flour

pinch of salt

½ tsp baking powder

2 tsp mixed spice

100 g/3½ oz granulated sugar

175 g/6 oz raisins

55 g/2 oz butter, melted, plus extra for greasing

1 egg, beaten

2 tbsp milk, plus extra if needed

caster sugar, for sprinkling

Gur Cake

This filling Dublin specialty is a good way to use up stale Madeira cake or sponge cake. It's traditionally eaten as a snack, but can also be served warm with cream or ice cream as a dessert.

METHOD

Preheat the oven to 190°C/375°F/Gas Mark 5. Grease a 30 x 18-cm/12 x 7-inch baking tin. Divide the pastry into two pieces, then roll out one piece and use to line the prepared tin.

Put the cake into a food processor and pulse until coarse crumbs form. Put the crumbs into a mixing bowl and add the flour, salt, baking powder, mixed spice, granulated sugar and raisins, mixing well to combine. Add the butter, egg and milk and mix until stiff.

Spread the mixture over the pastry in the tin, then roll out the remaining pastry and use to cover the cake. Slash the pastry lid with a sharp knife several times, then bake in the preheated oven for 50 minutes–1 hour until the pastry is crisp and golden.

Sprinkle with caster sugar and leave to cool in the tin, then cut into squares and serve.

MAKES 24 SQUARES

INGREDIENTS

225 g/8 oz butter,
plus extra for
greasing
300 ml/10 fl oz
water
225 g/8 oz soft light
brown sugar
450 g/1 lb raisins
450 g/1 lb currants
275 g/10 oz plain
flour
1 tsp baking powder
1 tsp mixed spice
4 eggs
150 ml/5 fl oz milk

Boiled Fruit Cake

This is probably the most popular of the
traditional Irish fruit cakes. It keeps well
and tastes best the day after baking.

METHOD

Preheat the oven to 190°C/375°F/Gas Mark 5. Grease a 20-cm/
8-inch round cake tin and line the base with baking paper.

Put the butter, water, sugar, raisins and currants into a medium-
sized saucepan over a low heat and bring to the boil, stirring to
dissolve the sugar. Boil for 10 minutes, then pour into a mixing
bowl and leave to cool slightly.

Sift the flour, baking powder and mixed spice into a separate
bowl. Beat the eggs with a little milk, then slowly add the egg
mixture to the cooled fruit mixture. Add the flour mixture with
as much milk as is needed to make a fairly stiff mixture.

Transfer the batter to the prepared tin and bake in the
preheated oven for 30 minutes. Reduce the oven temperature
to 160°C/325°F/Gas Mark 3 and bake for a further 30 minutes,
then reduce the oven temperature to 140°C/275°F/Gas Mark 1
and bake for a further 1 hour, until the cake is springy to the
touch and shrinking away from the side of the tin.

Leave to cool in the tin, then turn out and wrap in greaseproof
paper or foil and store in a tin.

SERVES 8-10

INGREDIENTS

butter, for greasing

175 g/6 oz soft light brown sugar

3 eggs

175 ml/6 fl oz sunflower oil

175 g/6 oz carrots, coarsely grated

2 very ripe bananas, mashed

55 g/2 oz chopped walnuts, plus extra to decorate

280 g/10 oz plain flour

1 tsp ground cinnamon

½ tsp salt

1 tsp bicarbonate of soda

2 tsp baking powder

Frosting

200 g/7 oz full-fat cream cheese

115 g/4 oz icing sugar

SERVES 8

Carrot Cake

This is not a traditional Irish bake, but it has become very popular in the last 30 years or so. It can be made with butter, but the texture is better when sunflower oil is used.

METHOD

Preheat the oven to 180°C/350°F/Gas Mark 4. Grease a 23-cm/9-inch round springform cake tin and line the base with baking paper.

Put the sugar, eggs, oil, carrots, bananas and walnuts into a mixing bowl. Sift in the flour, cinnamon, salt, bicarbonate of soda and baking powder and beat until smooth.

Pour the batter into the prepared tin and bake in the preheated oven for 1 hour 5 minutes until well risen and golden and a skewer inserted into the centre of the cake comes out clean. Leave to cool in the tin for 10 minutes, then unclip and release the springform, peel off the lining paper, transfer the cake to a wire rack and leave to cool completely.

To make the frosting, put the cheese into a mixing bowl and gradually add the icing sugar, beating well after each addition, until smooth. Spread the icing over the top of the cooled cake, decorate with chopped walnuts and leave in a cool place until the frosting has set slightly.

INGREDIENTS

100 g/3½ oz butter, softened

100 g/3½ oz caster sugar

100 g/3½ oz self-raising flour

1 tsp baking powder

2 eggs

Base/topping

55 g/2 oz butter, softened

55 g/2 oz soft light brown sugar

7 canned pineapple rings, drained, 2 tbsp syrup reserved

7 whole glacé cherries

Pineapple Upside-down Cake

This colourful cake is usually served at afternoon tea, but it also makes a good dessert, served warm with whipped cream or ice cream.

METHOD

Preheat the oven to 180°C/350°F/Gas Mark 4.

To make the base/topping, put the butter and sugar into a bowl and cream together until pale and fluffy. Spread over the base and a little way up the side of a 23-cm/9-inch round cake tin. Place a pineapple ring in the centre, then arrange the remaining six rings in a circle around it. Place a cherry in each ring.

Put the butter, sugar, flour, baking powder, eggs and reserved pineapple syrup into a mixing bowl and beat well until the mixture has a soft dropping consistency.

Spoon the mixture into the tin, levelling the top. Bake in the preheated oven for 35 minutes, then leave to cool in the tin for 5 minutes. Invert the tin over a serving plate and turn out the cake. Leave to cool or serve warm.

SERVES 6

INGREDIENTS

125 g/4½ oz
butter, plus extra for
greasing

125 g/4½ oz caster
sugar

125 g/4½ oz
marmalade

225 g/8 oz self-
raising flour

2 eggs, beaten

2 tbsp milk

icing sugar, for
dusting

Marmalade Cake

This delicious cut-and-come again cake
has a distinctly breakfasty flavour and is
good toasted and spread with butter.

METHOD

Preheat the oven to 190°C/375°F/Gas Mark 5. Grease a 20-cm/
8-inch round cake tin and line with foil.

Cream the butter and sugar together until pale and fluffy. Add
the marmalade and beat in well. Gradually add the flour, eggs
and milk and spread the mixture in the prepared tin, levelling
the top.

Bake in the preheated oven for 1 hour, then leave to cool in the
tin. Dust with icing sugar just before serving.

SERVES 6-8

Baking with Alcohol

Wine and spirits have been used in baking for centuries as a way of adding flavour and preserving cakes. Alcohol keeps baked goods moist and the addition of a healthy dose of spirits will preserve them for a relatively long time. It was an old Irish wedding tradition to keep the top tier of the wedding cake for the christening of the first child of the marriage, so the cake had to last for at least nine months!

While spirits – brandy or whiskey – are the most common alcoholic additions, stout (which is cheaper) is a time-honoured Irish tradition. Porter cake (see page 66) and Guinness chocolate cake (see page 114) are two perennial favourites. Stout is even added to Christmas pudding (see page 240), giving a rich dark flavour and colour to the festive dessert. Most people believe that the alcohol burns off during cooking – while this may be true in the case of pan-fried recipes, cakes, especially those that continue to be injected with spirits during storage, retain some of their alcohol content, although not enough that an elegant slice will make you tipsy!

Liqueurs are also used to add interesting flavour. Irish Mist is a longtime favourite (see page 94), while fruit-flavoured brandies and liqueurs such as triple sec and Tia Maria have all been given a successful whirl in Irish kitchens.

In 1974 there was an alcoholic sea change with the advent of the first of the Irish cream liqueurs, innovative emulsifications of whiskey and cream that have increased in popularity since they burst upon the drinking scene. They have been used to great effect in baking, used as one of the main components in delicious cheesecakes (see pages 124 and 156), as a substitute for cream in luxury versions of bread and butter pudding, and in fillings for macarons and frosting for cupcakes.

INGREDIENTS

300 g/10½ oz
butter, plus extra for
greasing

100 g/3½ oz cocoa
powder

150 ml/5 fl oz
Guinness

250 g/9 oz plain
flour

2 tsp bicarbonate
of soda

375 g/13 oz golden
caster sugar

3 large eggs, beaten

150 ml/5 fl oz
soured cream

2 tsp vanilla extract

Frosting

125 g/4½ oz butter,
softened

225 g/8 oz full-fat
cream cheese

225 g/8 oz icing
sugar

Guinness Chocolate Cake

**Guinness gives this delicious cake a depth
of unusual flavour. Great for a celebration.**

METHOD

Preheat the oven to 180°C/350°F/Gas Mark 4. Grease a 23-cm/
9-inch round loose-based cake tin and line the base with baking
paper. Put the butter into a saucepan over a medium heat and
heat until melted. Whisk in the cocoa powder and then the
Guinness. Remove from the heat.

Put the flour, bicarbonate of soda and caster sugar into a large
mixing bowl. Make a well in the centre and add the butter
mixture, then add the eggs, soured cream and vanilla extract.
Stir to combine thoroughly, then pour the batter into the
prepared tin and bake in the preheated oven for 1 hour, or until
a skewer inserted into the centre comes out clean (do keep an
eye on the cake – because of its dark colour it will be difficult to
tell if it's burning). Leave to cool in the tin for 10 minutes, then
turn out onto a wire rack and leave to cool completely.

Meanwhile, make the frosting. Put the butter into a bowl with
the cream cheese and beat well until light and creamy. Sift in
the icing sugar and beat until smooth. Spread the frosting over
the top of the cake and serve.

SERVES 8–10

INGREDIENTS

200 g/7 oz white self-raising flour

125 g/4½ oz butter, plus extra for greasing

85 g/3 oz sugar

1 tsp ground coriander

2 tsp ground cinnamon

55 g/2 oz mixed peel

1 Bramley apple, peeled, cored and thinly sliced

1 egg, beaten

2 tbsp milk

Apple Cinnamon Cake

This spiced cake has the unusual addition of ground coriander, which complements the pairing of apple and cinnamon.

METHOD

Preheat the oven to 200°C/400°F/Gas Mark 6. Grease a 20-cm/8-inch round cake tin.

Sift the flour into a mixing bowl, cut in the butter and rub into the flour. Stir in the sugar, coriander, cinnamon and mixed peel, then add the apple slices and mix to combine. Stir in the egg and milk. Knead lightly until the dough is smooth and elastic.

Place the dough in the prepared tin and bake in the preheated oven for 35 minutes, covering the top with tin foil if it begins to brown too quickly.

Leave to cool in the tin for 10 minutes, then turn out onto a wire cooling rack and leave to cool completely.

SERVES 6-8

INGREDIENTS

175 g/6 oz self-raising flour

165 g/5¾ oz caster sugar

1 tsp baking powder

125 g/4½ oz butter

3 eggs, beaten

2 tbsp milk

Madeira Cake

Despite its name, this plain, dense-textured cake contains no alcohol – it was intended to be eaten with a glass of Madeira wine or sherry.

METHOD

Preheat the oven to 200°C/400°F/Gas Mark 6. Grease a 450-g/1-lb loaf tin and line with baking paper.

Sift the flour and sugar into a mixing bowl and add the baking powder. Put the butter into a separate bowl and cream until light and fluffy.

Add the flour mixture to the butter, then add the eggs and milk and beat well for 3 minutes.

Put the batter into the prepared tin, levelling the top, and bake in the preheated oven for 1 hour, or until golden and a skewer inserted into the centre comes out clean. Leave to cool in the tin for 5–10 minutes, then turn out onto a wire rack and leave to cool completely.

SERVES 6-8

INGREDIENTS

250 g/9 oz plain flour, plus extra for dusting

2 tsp baking powder

½ tsp salt

200 g/7 oz caster sugar

125 g/4½ oz butter, softened, plus extra for greasing

2 eggs

1 tsp vanilla extract

250 ml/9 fl oz milk

2 tbsp cocoa powder

Marble Cake

This is a variation on plain Madeira cake – don't mix in the dark batter too vigorously, or you'll spoil the effect.

METHOD

Preheat the oven to 180°C/325°F/Gas Mark 4. Grease a 23-cm/9-inch cake tin and dust with flour, shaking out any excess.

Put all the ingredients, except the cocoa powder, into a mixing bowl and beat with a hand-held electric mixer until smooth. Pour all but 175 g/6 oz of the batter into the prepared tin.

Stir the cocoa powder into the remaining batter, then use a dessert spoon to drop it onto the batter in the tin. Use a knife to swirl the two batters together very lightly, so that you get a marbled effect.

Bake in the preheated oven for 30–35 minutes, or until a skewer inserted into the centre of the cake comes out clean. Leave to cool in the tin for 10 minutes, then turn out onto a wire rack and leave to cool completely.

SERVES 8-10

TARTS,
CRUMBLES
& PIES

INGREDIENTS

660 g/1 lb 8 oz full-fat cream cheese

250 g/9 oz caster sugar

25 g/1 oz cocoa powder, plus extra for dusting

3 tbsp plain flour

3 eggs

125 ml/4 fl oz soured cream

4 tbsp Bailey's Irish Cream liqueur

Base

200 g/7 oz digestive biscuits, crushed

40 g/1½ oz icing sugar

35 g/1¼ oz cocoa powder

100 g/3½ oz butter, melted

Bailey's Chocolate Cheesecake

This indulgent baked cheesecake is a perfect dessert for a celebration meal.

METHOD

Preheat the oven to 180°C/350°F/Gas Mark 4. To make the base, put the crushed biscuits, icing sugar and cocoa powder into a mixing bowl, add the butter and stir to combine.

Press into the base of a 23-cm/9-inch round springform cake tin and bake in the preheated oven for 10 minutes. Set aside and increase the oven temperature to 230°C/450°F/Gas Mark 8.

Put the cream cheese, caster sugar, cocoa powder and flour into a mixing bowl and beat with a hand-held electric mixer until smooth. Add the eggs one at a time, beating well after each addition. Add the soured cream and liqueur and beat until well combined.

Pour the mixture into the tin and bake for 10 minutes, then reduce the oven temperature to 120°C/250°F/Gas Mark ½ and bake for a further 1 hour.

Use a knife to loosen the cake from the side of the tin, then leave to cool completely. Unclip and remove the springform (don't worry if the surface of the cake cracks a little) and chill in the fridge for a few hours. Dust with cocoa powder just before serving.

SERVES 12

INGREDIENTS

225 g/8 oz ready-made shortcrust pastry

3 eggs

450 g/1 lb curd cheese or cottage cheese

4 tbsp caster sugar

25 g/1 oz butter, softened, plus extra for greasing

finely grated zest and juice of 1 small lemon

1 tsp vanilla extract

1 tbsp plain flour, plus extra for dusting

Irish Curd Tart

Curd cheese gives this baked cheesecake a good texture. You could use cottage cheese instead.

METHOD

Preheat the oven to 180°C/350°F/Gas Mark 4 and grease a 20-cm/8-inch round loose-based tart tin. Roll out the pastry on a work surface lightly dusted with flour, then use to line the prepared tin.

Separate 2 of the eggs and beat the yolks, then whisk the whites until they hold stiff peaks. Put the cheese, 3 tablespoons of the sugar, half the butter and the egg yolks into a bowl and mix to combine.

Stir in the lemon zest and juice and the vanilla extract. Beat well, then gradually fold in the egg whites.

Spread the filling evenly in the pastry case. Melt the remaining butter and mix with the remaining egg and sugar and the flour. Spread the mixture evenly over the filling.

Bake in the preheated oven for 35–40 minutes, or until golden brown. Leave to cool in the tin, then turn out, cut into wedges and serve.

SERVES 6-8

INGREDIENTS

butter, for greasing

plain flour, for dusting

250 g/9 oz ready-made shortcrust pastry

450 g/9 oz jam

milk, for brushing

whipped cream or custard, to serve

Jam Tart

This is a great standby dessert for unexpected guests. You can use any jam, but one that provides a good colour contrast with the pastry is best.

METHOD

Preheat the oven to 200°C/400°F/Gas Mark 6 and grease a 20-cm/8-inch tart tin.

Roll out the pastry on a work surface lightly dusted with flour and use to line the prepared tin. Chill in the fridge until needed. Re-roll the pastry trimmings and cut out 8 strips, each slightly longer than the diameter of the tin.

Heat the jam over a low heat until warm, then spread over the pastry case. Weave the pastry strips in a lattice pattern over the top, pressing the ends into the edge of the pastry case. Brush with a little milk.

Bake in the preheated oven for about 30 minutes until the pastry is golden. Leave to cool in the tin for 30 minutes, then cut into wedges and serve with whipped cream.

SERVES 6-8

INGREDIENTS

butter, for greasing

flour, for dusting

250 g/9 oz ready-made shortcrust pastry

1 large egg

4 large egg yolks

150 g/5½ oz caster sugar

finely grated zest and juice of 4 lemons

150 ml/5 fl oz double cream

Easy Lemon Tart

This popular tart has been borrowed from the French tradition and simplified.

METHOD

Grease a 23-cm/9-inch loose-based tart tin. Roll out the pastry on a work surface lightly dusted with flour and use to line the tin. Chill in the fridge for 30 minutes.

Meanwhile, preheat the oven to 190°C/375°F/Gas Mark 5. Prick the base of the pastry case, line with baking paper and fill with baking beans, then bake in the preheated oven for 10 minutes. Remove the paper and beans, return to the oven and bake for a further 8–10 minutes. Reduce the oven temperature to 160°C/325°F/Gas Mark 3.

Put the egg, egg yolks and sugar into a jug and beat until smooth. Stir in the lemon zest and juice and the cream and mix to combine.

Put the tin in the oven, carefully pour in the filling and bake for 25–30 minutes. Leave to cool for 15 minutes, then serve warm, or leave to cool completely and chill until ready to serve.

SERVES 8

INGREDIENTS

flour, for dusting

375 g/13 oz ready-made puff pastry

5 Bramley apples, peeled, cored and thinly sliced

juice of 1 lemon

25 g/1 oz butter, diced

2 tbsp caster sugar

3 tbsp apricot jam, for glazing

ice cream or custard, to serve

Open Apple Tart

A rustic-looking apple tart that's quick and easy to prepare.

METHOD

Preheat the oven to 220°C/425°F/Gas Mark 7. Line a baking sheet with baking paper.

Roll out the pastry to a 35-cm/14-inch round on a work surface lightly dusted with flour and place on the prepared baking sheet.

Toss the apples in the lemon juice and spread them over the pastry to within 2 cm/¾ inch of the edge. Raise the edge of the pastry and fold it over the outer ring of apples to make a rim. Dot with butter, sprinkle with sugar and bake in the preheated oven for 20–25 minutes until the apples are tender and the pastry is golden.

Heat the jam in a small saucepan over a medium heat and pass through a small sieve to remove the fruit pieces. Brush the apples and pastry rim with the glaze and serve the tart hot.

SERVES 6-8

INGREDIENTS

butter, for greasing

plain flour, for dusting

250 g/9 oz ready-made shortcrust pastry

150 g/5 oz fresh white breadcrumbs

225 ml/8 fl oz golden syrup

beaten egg, for brushing

golden caster sugar, for sprinkling

whipped cream or vanilla ice cream, to serve

Golden Syrup Tart

Golden syrup has so many uses in home baking that many people keep a tin on standby in the storecupboard.

METHOD

Preheat the oven to 180°C/350°F/Gas Mark 4. Grease a 20-cm/8-inch round loose-based tart tin.

Roll out the pastry on a work surface lightly dusted with flour and use to line the prepared tin.

Mix the breadcrumbs and golden syrup together and spread evenly in the pastry case.

Bake in the preheated oven for 20 minutes. Brush the pastry edges with beaten egg and sprinkle the tart with sugar, then return to the oven for a further 15 minutes, or until the pastry is golden.

Leave to cool for 15–20 minutes, then cut into wedges and serve with cream.

SERVES 6-8

INGREDIENTS

plain flour, for
dusting

300 g/10½ oz
ready-made
shortcrust pastry

150 g/5½ oz golden
caster sugar, plus
extra for dusting

½ tsp cinnamon

1 kg/2 lb 4 oz
Bramley apples,
cored, peeled and
thickly sliced

beaten egg white,
for brushing

whipped cream or
vanilla ice cream, to
serve

Apple Pie

Apple pie is the ultimate comfort food
dessert. This one is full of succulent
Bramley apples and is delicious served
with lots of whipped cream.

METHOD

Preheat the oven to 190°C/375°F/Gas Mark 5. Cut off a third of
the pastry and set aside until needed. Roll out the remaining
pastry on a work surface lightly dusted with flour and use to
line a 20-cm/8-inch deep pie tin, leaving an overhang.

Mix the sugar and cinnamon together in a large bowl, then toss
the apples in the mixture. Put the apples into the tin.

Roll out the reserved pastry to a round about 2.5 cm/1 inch
larger than the diameter of the top of the tin. Brush some cold
water around the pastry rim, then lay the pastry round on top,
crimping the edges to seal. Pierce the pastry about five times to
allow the steam to escape during baking.

Brush the pie with the egg white and dust with sugar. Bake in
the preheated oven for 40–45 minutes until golden. Dust with
sugar, then serve with whipped cream or ice cream.

SERVES 6-8

and tarts. Delicious wild fraughans (bilberries) can be foraged in the countryside in July and August – they are smaller and sweeter than their close relative, the blueberry, and are great baked in muffins and buns.

Late summer brings pears – their juicy sweetness means that you don't have to add too much sugar when baking with them, and their flavour is a perfect complement to chocolate (see page 148) and almonds (see page 150). They look decorative when sliced vertically and arranged artistically, making them ideal for open tarts served as desserts or for afternoon tea.

Autumn fruit

Autumn is the season of crisp apples and lip-staining blackberries foraged from the hedgerows – crumble, pies, tarts, muffins and biscuits can be made using this fruity match made in heaven. The best type of cooking apple is one that breaks down when heated – Bramleys are the perfect 'cookers'. Eating apples are not recommended as baking apples as they are often mealy and bland-tasting when cooked.

INGREDIENTS

225 g/8 oz
blackberries, picked
over

450 g/1 lb Bramley
apples, peeled,
cored and sliced

100 g/3½ oz
granulated sugar

100 g/3½ oz plain
flour

55 g/2 oz porridge
oats

85 g/3 oz butter,
plus extra for
greasing

100 g/3½ oz
demerara sugar

ice cream, to serve

Autumn Crumble

This mellow crumble makes the most
of two of autumn's most plentiful fruity
offerings – apples and blackberries.

METHOD

Preheat the oven to 180°C/350°F/Gas Mark 4. Grease a
1.2-litre/2-pint baking dish.

Put the blackberries, apples and granulated sugar into the
prepared dish and stir to combine.

Put the flour, oats, butter and demerara sugar into a mixing
bowl and rub together until coarse crumbs form. Spread evenly
over the fruit mixture, pressing down slightly, then bake in the
preheated oven for 40 minutes until the topping is browned
and the fruit juices are bubbling up at the sides.

Serve hot, with ice cream.

SERVES 4–6

INGREDIENTS

450 g/1 lb trimmed rhubarb, cut into 2.5-cm/1-inch lengths

100 g/3½ oz caster sugar

150 g/5½ oz plain flour

85 g/3 oz butter, at room temperature

55 g/2 oz demerara sugar

5-cm/2-inch piece fresh ginger, grated

55 g/2 oz hazelnuts, finely chopped

custard, to serve

Rhubarb & Ginger Crumble

The rhubarb season is very short, so make sure you take advantage of it with this delicious crumble.

METHOD

Put the rhubarb into a saucepan with the caster sugar and 2–3 tablespoons of water and cook over a low heat for about 15 minutes, until soft but not disintegrating. Transfer to a baking dish.

Meanwhile, preheat the oven to 200°C/400°F/Gas Mark 6. Sift the flour into a bowl, cut in the butter and rub it in with your fingertips until coarse crumbs form.

Add the demerara sugar, ginger and nuts and mix to combine, then sprinkle the crumble over the rhubarb.

Bake in the preheated oven for 30 minutes and serve hot, with custard.

SERVES 6

INGREDIENTS

450 g/1 lb ready-made shortcrust pastry

250 g/9 oz caster sugar, plus extra for sprinkling

6 tbsp plain flour, plus extra for dusting

500 g/1 lb 2 oz trimmed rhubarb, chopped

½ tsp vanilla bean paste

Vanilla Rhubarb Pie

The warm sweetness of vanilla is a perfect foil for the sharp flavour of rhubarb.

METHOD

Preheat the oven to 230°C/450°F/Gas Mark 8. Divide the pastry into two pieces. Roll out one piece on a work surface lightly dusted with flour and use to line a 23-cm/9-inch pie dish.

Combine the sugar and flour in a bowl and spread a quarter of the mixture over the pastry in the pie dish. Pile in the rhubarb, dot with the vanilla bean paste and cover with the remaining flour mixture.

Roll out the second piece of pastry and place on top of the pie dish, trimming the edge and crimping it to seal. Use a sharp knife to cut a few slits in the pastry to allow the steam to escape during cooking.

Sprinkle with sugar and bake on the bottom shelf of the preheated oven for 15 minutes, then reduce the oven temperature to 180°C/350°F/Gas Mark 4 and cook for a further 40–45 minutes. Serve warm or cold.

SERVES 8

INGREDIENTS

butter, for greasing

plain flour, for dusting

250 g/9 oz ready-made shortcrust pastry

150 g/5½ oz plain chocolate

2 eggs, beaten

1 tbsp single cream

2 large ripe pears

whipped cream, to serve

Chocolate & Pear Tart

Use a good quality chocolate with a high percentage of cocoa solids to complement the sweetness of the pears.

METHOD

Preheat the oven to 180°C/350°F/Gas Mark 4. Grease a 20-cm/ 8-inch round loose-based tart tin.

Roll out the pastry on a work surface lightly dusted with flour and use to line the tart tin. Line with baking paper and fill with baking beans, then bake in the preheated oven for 15 minutes. Remove from the oven and increase the oven temperature to 190°C/375°F/Gas Mark 5.

Put the chocolate into a bowl set over a saucepan of gently simmering water and heat until melted. Remove from the heat and leave to cool slightly, then beat in the eggs. Fold in the cream. Spread the mixture over the base of the pastry case.

Peel and core the pears and cut them lengthways into thin slices. Arrange the pear slices on the chocolate in an overlapping pattern and sprinkle over the caster sugar.

Bake for about 25 minutes until the pears are golden brown. Leave to cool completely, then serve with whipped cream.

SERVES 6

Pear & Almond Tart

This luscious tart has a sweet pastry and is particularly good when made with firm pears. The almonds give it a lovely texture.

INGREDIENTS

Pastry
85 g/3 oz chilled butter, diced, plus extra for greasing
175 g/6 oz plain flour, plus extra for dusting
25 g/1 oz caster sugar
1 egg

Filling
2 eggs
100 g/3½ oz caster sugar
3 firm pears, peeled and halved
100 g/3½ oz ground almonds
25 g/1 oz butter, melted
55 g/2 oz self-raising flour

METHOD

To make the pastry, rub the butter into the flour until fine crumbs form. Add the sugar and mix to combine, then add the egg and mix until the dough comes together. Add a little water if necessary. Leave to stand for at least 1 hour.

Preheat the oven to 180°C/325°F/Gas Mark 4. Grease a 20-cm/8-inch round loose-based tart tin. Roll out the pastry on a work surface lightly dusted with flour and use to line the prepared tin. Prick the base with a fork and chill in the fridge until needed.

To make the filling, put the eggs and sugar into a bowl and whisk with a hand-held electric mixer until pale and creamy. Fold in the almonds, then mix in the butter. Add the flour and mix to combine.

Spread some of the almond mixture in the pastry case, then arrange the pears on top. Top with the remaining almond mixture and bake in the preheated oven for about 40 minutes. Serve warm.

SERVES 6

INGREDIENTS

butter, for greasing
flour, for dusting
250 g/9 oz
ready-made sweet
shortcrust pastry
400 ml/14 fl oz
double cream
140 g/5 oz plain
chocolate, roughly
chopped
2 tbsp whiskey
2 tbsp icing sugar
white chocolate
curls, to decorate

Chocolate Whiskey Mousse Tart

A rich tart that should be served after a light meal – the whiskey is just a suggestion but it adds a great aroma.

METHOD

Preheat the oven to 200°C/400°F/Gas Mark 6. Grease a 23-cm/9-inch round tart tin.

Roll out the pastry on a work surface lightly dusted with flour and use to line the prepared tin. Prick the pastry case with a fork, then line with baking paper, fill with baking beans and bake in the preheated oven for 10 minutes. Remove the paper and beans and bake for a further 2 minutes, then leave to cool in the tin.

Meanwhile, put 175 ml/6 fl oz of the cream into a saucepan and bring to a simmer over a low heat. Remove from the heat and add the chocolate, stirring until melted and combined. Leave to cool to room temperature, then stir in the whiskey.

Whip the remaining cream with the icing sugar until stiff peaks form. Gently fold in the chocolate mixture until combined.

Pour the chocolate filling into the pastry case and chill for 1½ hours, or until set. Serve chilled, decorated with white chocolate curls. The tart will keep in the fridge for up to 2 days.

SERVES 8-10

INGREDIENTS

butter, for greasing
250 g/9 oz ready-made shortcrust pastry
350 ml/12 fl oz milk
4 large egg yolks
100 g/3½ oz caster sugar
1 tbsp plain flour, plus extra for dusting
1 tbsp cornflour
½ tsp vanilla extract
3 tbsp apricot jam
1 tsp water
600 g/1 lb 5 oz strawberries, hulled and sliced

Strawberry Tart

Custard provides a creamy base for strawberries in this classic summer tart.

METHOD

Preheat the oven to 190°C/375°F/Gas Mark 5. Grease a 23-cm/ 9-inch round loose-based tart tin. Roll out the pastry on a work surface lightly dusted with flour and use to line the prepared tin. Prick the pastry case all over with a fork, line with baking paper and fill with baking beans, then bake in the preheated oven for 15 minutes. Remove the paper and beans and bake for a further 5 minutes. Leave to cool.

Heat the milk to just below boiling point, then leave to cool slightly. Put the egg yolks into a bowl with the sugar and whisk until thick and pale. Add the flour and cornflour and whisk until smooth, then gradually add the milk, whisking constantly.

Pour into a clean saucepan and heat over a medium heat, stirring until beginning to thicken, then reduce the heat to low and simmer, stirring until thick. Stir in the vanilla extract, spread the custard in the pastry case and chill in the fridge for 5 hours, or until set.

Heat the jam in a small saucepan with the water, then pass through a sieve to remove the fruit. Arrange the strawberry slices on the custard, brush with the apricot glaze and serve.

SERVES 6

Irish Cream Cheesecake

INGREDIENTS

85 g/3 oz butter, melted

225 g/8 oz digestive biscuit crumbs

700 g/1 lb 9 oz cream cheese, softened

115 g/4 oz sugar

3 eggs, beaten

2 tbsp plain flour

225 ml/8 fl oz Irish cream liqueur

1 tsp vanilla extract

This plain cheesecake is given a luxurious touch with the addition of a healthy glug of Irish cream liqueur.

METHOD

Preheat the oven to 180°C/350°F/Gas Mark 4. Mix the butter and biscuit crumbs together and press into the base of a 20-cm/8-inch round springform cake tin. Bake in the preheated oven for 5 minutes. Remove from the oven (do not switch off the oven).

Meanwhile, put the cheese and sugar into a bowl and mix to combine, then add the eggs, flour, liqueur and vanilla extract and beat until smooth.

Pour the mixture onto the crumb base, return to the oven and bake for 40 minutes. Leave to cool, then chill overnight.

SERVES 8-10

INGREDIENTS

butter, for greasing

flour, for dusting

250 g/9 oz ready-
made shortcrust
pastry

2 large eggs

200 ml/7 fl oz
double cream

85 g/3 oz caster
sugar

1 tsp vanilla extract

300 g/10½ oz
gooseberries, topped
and tailed

Gooseberry Tart

This easy tart is a luscious way of using up
some of the summer glut of gooseberries.

METHOD

Preheat the oven to 190°C/375°F/Gas Mark 5. Grease a 23-cm/
9-inch round loose-based tart tin. Roll out the pastry on a work
surface lightly dusted with flour and use to line the prepared
tin. Prick the pastry case all over with a fork.

Line the pastry case with baking paper and baking beans and
bake blind in the preheated oven for 15 minutes. Remove the
paper and beans and bake for a further 5 minutes. Leave to
cool. Do not switch off the oven.

Meanwhile, put the eggs, cream, sugar and vanilla extract into a
large jug and beat well together.

Arrange the gooseberries on the pastry case and pour over the
egg mixture. Bake for 35–40 minutes until the custard is set.
Serve warm or cold.

SERVES 6

INGREDIENTS

1 kg/2 lb 4 oz gooseberries, topped and tailed

3 tbsp water

55 g/2 oz caster sugar

55 g/2 oz plain white flour

25 g/1 oz wholemeal flour

55 g/2 oz chilled butter, diced

55 g/2 oz soft light brown sugar

25 g/1 oz porridge oats

25 g/1 oz chopped hazelnuts

Gooseberry & Hazelnut Crumble

A delicious combination of contrasts – tart and sweet, soft and crunchy – this is a great summer dessert.

METHOD

Preheat the oven to 200°C/400°F/Gas Mark 6. Put the gooseberries into a large saucepan with 2 tablespoons of the water and heat gently until they are beginning to release their juices. Add the caster sugar, stirring to dissolve, then pour into a large baking dish.

Sift the white flour and wholemeal flour into a mixing bowl. Rub in the butter until coarse crumbs form. Add the brown sugar, oats and nuts and stir to combine.

Spoon the crumble mixture over the gooseberries and bake in the preheated oven for 20–25 minutes. Serve hot or warm.

SERVES 6

INGREDIENTS

Pastry

85 g/3 oz chilled butter, diced, plus extra for greasing

175 g/6 oz plain flour, plus extra for dusting

25 g/1 oz caster sugar

1 egg

Filling

2 eggs

100 g/3½ oz caster sugar

3 large apples, peeled, cored and halved

100 g/3½ oz ground almonds

25 g/1 oz butter, melted

55 g/2 oz self-raising flour

Apple & Almond Tart

This delicious tart is crisp outside with a soft and fruity filling.

METHOD

To make the pastry, rub the butter into the flour until fine crumbs form. Add the sugar and mix to combine, then add the egg and mix until the dough comes together, adding a little water if necessary. Leave to stand for at least 1 hour.

Preheat the oven to 180°C/325°F/Gas Mark 4. Grease a 20-cm/8-inch round loose-based tart tin. Roll out the pastry on a work surface lightly dusted with flour and use to line the prepared tin. Prick the pastry case all over with a fork and chill in the fridge until needed.

To make the filling, put the eggs and sugar into a bowl and whisk with a hand-held electric mixer until pale and creamy. Fold in the almonds, then mix in the butter. Add the flour and mix to combine.

Spread some of the almond mixture in the pastry case, then arrange the apple halves on top. Top with the remaining almond mixture and bake in the preheated oven for about 40 minutes. Serve warm.

SERVES 6

INGREDIENTS

butter, for greasing
flour, for dusting
250 g/9 oz ready-
made shortcrust
pastry
300 ml/10 fl oz milk
1 tbsp cornflour
1 tbsp caster sugar
2 egg yolks
juice and grated zest
of 1 large lemon

Meringue
2 egg whites
115 g/4 oz caster
sugar

Lemon Meringue Pie

This classic dessert is very simple to make. The meringue should be soft and a bit chewy, not so hard that it turns to dust when you bite into it.

METHOD

Preheat the oven to 190°C/375°F/Gas Mark 5. Grease a 20-cm/ 8-inch cake tin. Roll out the pastry on a work surface lightly dusted with flour and use to line the prepared tin. Prick with a fork several times, line with baking paper and fill with baking beans, then bake in the preheated oven for 15 minutes. Remove the paper and beans. Do not switch off the oven.

Meanwhile, mix a little of the milk with the cornflour in a mixing bowl. Heat the remaining milk in a saucepan and pour it into the cornflour mixture, then return to the pan, bring to the boil and cook for 3–4 minutes, stirring constantly. Remove from the heat and add the sugar. Leave to cool slightly, then beat in the egg yolks and the lemon juice and zest. Pour the filling into the pastry case and bake for 5 minutes until set. Reduce the oven temperature to 150°C/300°F/Gas Mark 2.

To make the meringue, whisk the egg whites until they hold stiff peaks, then whisk in 2 teaspoons of the sugar. Fold in the remaining sugar very carefully. Pile on top of the filling, covering it completely, and bake in the oven for 30 minutes until browned. Serve warm or chilled.

SERVES 6

INGREDIENTS

flour, for dusting

250 g/9 oz ready-made shortcrust pastry

4 large apples, peeled, cored and cut into chunks

2 tbsp water

juice of 1 lemon

85 g/2 oz caster sugar

3 large eggs, separated

Apple Amber

The meringue is very sweet, so use a tart apple, such as Bramley.

METHOD

Preheat the oven to 190°C/375°F/Gas Mark 5. Roll out the pastry on a work surface lightly dusted with flour and use to line a 20-cm/8-inch pie tin. Prick a few times with a fork, line with baking paper and fill with baking beans, then bake in the preheated oven for 15 minutes. Remove from the oven and take out the paper and beans. Reduce the oven temperature to 180°C/350°F/Gas Mark 4.

Put the apples and water into a large saucepan and heat over a medium heat until the apples have broken down (do not be tempted to add more water). Remove from the heat.

Beat the egg yolks. Add the lemon and three-quarters of the sugar to the apple, then add the egg yolks and stir. Spoon the mixture into the pastry case and bake for 20 minutes.

Meanwhile, whisk the egg whites until they hold stiff peaks, then gradually whisk in the remaining sugar. Pile on top of the filling, covering it completely, and bake in the oven for 10 minutes, or until browned. Serve warm or chilled.

SERVES 6

INGREDIENTS

Pastry

175 g/6 oz plain flour, plus extra for dusting

85 g/3 oz icing sugar

100 g/3½ oz chilled butter, diced, plus extra for greasing

1 large egg yolk

Filling

100 g/3½ oz butter, softened

100 g/3½ oz caster sugar

3 eggs, beaten

100 g/3½ oz ground almonds

55 g/2 oz plain flour

¼ tsp almond extract

250 g/9 oz raspberry jam

25 g/1 oz flaked almonds

SERVES 6-8

Bakewell Tart

This jam tart is an old favourite – it makes a great standby dessert or a classic afternoon tea cake.

METHOD

To make the pastry, put the flour and icing sugar into a food processor and pulse to combine. Add the butter and pulse until fine crumbs form. Add the egg yolk and pulse until the pastry comes together. Shape into a ball, wrap in clingfilm and chill in the fridge for up to 1 hour.

Preheat the oven to 180°C/350°F/Gas Mark 4 and preheat a baking sheet. Grease a 20-cm/8-inch loose-based tart tin. To make the filling, cream the butter and caster sugar until pale and fluffy, then beat in the eggs until smooth. Add the ground almonds, flour and almond extract and stir until combined.

Roll out the pastry on a work surface lightly dusted with flour and use to line the prepared tin. Spread the jam over the base of the pastry case, then cover with the batter, distributing it evenly and levelling until smooth. Sprinkle over the flaked almonds and bake in the preheated oven for 30–35 minutes until golden brown. Serve warm or cold.

INGREDIENTS

butter, for greasing

85 g/3 oz caster sugar

3 eggs, beaten

85 g/3 oz plain flour, plus extra for dusting

1 tbsp raspberry jam

400 g/14 oz fresh sliced fruit, such as peaches and strawberries

whipped cream, to serve

Fruit Flan

In the 1960s and 1970s fruit flan was usually made with a ready-made flan case and canned fruit. It's easy to make a case from scratch, and using fresh fruit makes it at least ten times more delicious.

METHOD

Preheat the oven to 200°C/400°F/Gas Mark 6. Grease a 20-cm/8-inch flan tin and dust it with flour, shaking out any excess.

Put the sugar and eggs into a bowl set over a saucepan of gently simmering water and whisk until pale and creamy.

Remove from the heat and gradually sift in the flour, folding it in with a metal spoon.

Pour the batter into the prepared tin and bake in the preheated oven for 10–15 minutes until golden.

Leave to cool in the tin for 10 minutes, then turn out onto a wire rack and leave to cool completely. Spread the jam on the base of the sponge, then fill with fruit and serve immediately with whipped cream.

SERVES 6-8

INGREDIENTS

Pastry

225 g/8 oz plain white flour, plus extra for dusting

pinch of salt

150 g/5 oz chilled butter, diced

1 egg yolk, beaten

Filling

450 g/1 lb potatoes

2 tbsp chopped fresh parsley

2 tbsp snipped fresh chives

3 hard-boiled eggs, sliced

4 bacon rashers, fried

salt

Donegal Pie

A filling savoury pie that makes good use of everyday ingredients. It tastes great cold, so it's a good choice for a packed lunch or picnic.

METHOD

To make the pastry, put the flour and salt into a bowl and rub in the butter until coarse crumbs form. Add the egg and as much water as is needed to mix to a soft but firm dough. Turn out onto a work surface lightly dusted with flour and knead for 1–2 minutes. Set aside until ready to assemble the pie.

To make the filling, steam the potatoes and mash well. Mix in the parsley and chives and add salt to taste. Line the base of a pie dish with half the potatoes and place a layer of egg slices on top. Cut the bacon into small pieces and scatter over the egg with any of the fat from frying. Spread the remaining potato mixture over the bacon.

Meanwhile, preheat the oven to 200°C/400°F/Gas Mark 6. Roll out the pastry with a floured rolling pin and use to cover the pie. Bake in the preheated oven for 25–30 minutes, covering with foil after 10 minutes. Serve hot or cold.

SERVES 6-8

INGREDIENTS

650 g/1 lb 7 oz white fish fillets, skinned

250 g/9 oz cooked, peeled prawns (optional)

200 g/7 oz spinach, cooked, drained and finely chopped

55 g/2 oz butter, plus extra for greasing

1 onion, finely chopped

150 ml/5 fl oz single cream

1 tbsp English mustard powder

juice of 1 lemon

creamy mashed potatoes, for topping

salt and freshly ground black pepper

Fish Pie

When cod was plentiful it was the traditional ingredient in this pie, but you could use any other firm white fish. Prawns are not strictly necessary, but add lovely colour, flavour and texture.

METHOD

Preheat the oven to 180°C/350°F/Gas Mark 4. Grease a 2-litre/3½-pint baking dish.

Cut the fish into bite-sized pieces and place in the base of the prepared dish. Scatter over the prawns, if using, and the spinach and season to taste with salt and pepper.

Melt the butter in a saucepan, add the onion and fry over a medium heat until softened. Add the cream and mustard powder and slowly stir in the lemon juice. Bring to the boil, stirring, then remove from the heat.

Pour the mixture into the dish, making sure that the fish and prawns are evenly covered.

Pipe the mashed potatoes onto the fish mixture, then bake in the preheated oven for 15–20 minutes until the topping is golden. Serve immediately.

SERVES 6

INGREDIENTS

Pastry

350 g/12 oz plain flour, plus extra for dusting

pinch of salt

25 g/1 oz butter

2 egg yolks, beaten

water, for mixing

milk, for brushing

Filling

350 g/12 oz lamb shoulder, trimmed and cubed

2 tbsp chopped fresh marjoram

2 tbsp snipped fresh chives

4 tbsp lamb stock

salt

Dingle Pie

A tasty and very filling lamb pie that is great for picnics.

METHOD

Preheat the oven to 200°C/400°F/Gas Mark 6.

To make the pastry, put the flour and salt into a mixing bowl and rub in the butter until coarse crumbs form. Add the egg and as much water as is needed to mix to a soft but firm dough. Turn out onto a work surface lightly dusted with flour and knead for 1–2 minutes.

Divide the dough into two pieces and roll out each piece to a round with a diameter of about 20 cm/8 inches. Use one round to line a pie dish, then add the lamb, season to taste with salt and scatter over the marjoram and chives. Sprinkle over the stock, then place the second pastry round on top and crimp the edges to seal. Brush with milk and slash the pastry lid a few times to allow the steam to escape during cooking.

Bake in the preheated oven for 20 minutes, then cover the pie with foil, reduce the oven temperature to 180°C/350°F/Gas Mark 4 and bake for a further 45 minutes. Serve hot or cold.

SERVES 8

INGREDIENTS

butter, for greasing

plain flour, for
dusting

250 g/9 oz ready-
made shortcrust
pastry

6 streaky bacon
rashers, chopped

4 large eggs

½ tsp salt

¼ tsp freshly ground
black pepper

100 g/3½ oz mature
Cheddar cheese,
coarsely grated

1 onion, roughly
chopped

Bacon & Egg Flan

You can make a subtle alteration to the
flavour by using smoked bacon rashers.

METHOD

Preheat the oven to 220°C/425°F/Gas Mark 7. Grease a 23-cm/
9-inch flan tin.

Roll out the pastry on a work surface lightly dusted with flour
and use to line the prepared tin, trimming the pastry 2.5 cm/
1 inch above the top of the tin. Line with baking paper, fill with
baking beans and bake in the preheated oven for 10 minutes.
Remove the paper and bake for a further 2 minutes.

Meanwhile, add the bacon to a hot frying pan and fry until
cooked to your liking. Beat the eggs with the salt and pepper.

Remove the pastry case from the oven and reduce the oven
temperature to 150°C/325°F/Gas Mark 3. Sprinkle the bacon,
most of the cheese and the onion over the base of the pastry
case. Pour in the egg mixture and sprinkle with the remaining
cheese.

Return the flan to the oven and bake for 45–50 minutes. Serve
warm or cold.

SERVES 4–6

INGREDIENTS

Filling

675 g/1 lb 8 oz
stewing steak,
trimmed and cubed

225 g/8 oz beef
kidneys, chopped

flour, for dusting

2 tbsp chopped fresh
thyme

2 tbsp chopped fresh
marjoram

125 ml/4 fl oz
Guinness

salt and freshly
ground black pepper

Pastry

275 g/9¾ oz plain
flour, plus extra for
dusting

pinch of salt

175 g/6 oz butter

2 egg yolks, beaten

milk, for brushing

Steak & Kidney Pie with Guinness

This hearty, rib-sticking pie will warm you up on the coldest day. The Guinness loses its bitterness in the cooking and adds a subtle depth of flavour.

METHOD

Preheat the oven to 200°C/400°F/Gas Mark 6.

Put the steak and kidneys into a large bowl, add some flour and toss to coat. Arrange in a pie dish, add the thyme, marjoram and salt and pepper to taste and pour in the Guinness. Set aside while you prepare the pastry.

Put the flour and salt into a mixing bowl and rub in the butter until coarse crumbs form. Add the egg and as much water as is needed to mix to a soft but firm dough. Turn out the pastry onto a work surface lightly dusted with flour and knead for 1–2 minutes. Roll out and place over the meat, with an upturned egg cup placed in the centre of the dish to support the weight of the pastry. Trim the edges.

Reroll the pastry trimmings and cut out leaves to decorate the top of the pie. Brush with milk and bake in the preheated oven for 15–20 minutes. Reduce the oven temperature to 150°C/300°F/Gas Mark 2 and bake for a further 2 hours, covering with foil to prevent the pastry drying out.

SERVES 6-8

INGREDIENTS

Pastry

300 g/10½ oz
self-raising flour, plus
extra for dusting

125 g/4½ oz butter

85 g/3 oz mashed
potatoes

pinch of salt

1 egg, beaten

milk, for brushing

Filling

1 chicken, boned
and cut into pieces

flour, for dusting

vegetable oil and
butter, for frying

3 tomatoes, peeled
and chopped

1 tbsp chopped fresh
parsley

1 tbsp snipped fresh
chives

4 tbsp Guinness

4 lean bacon rashers,
cut into strips

Chicken Pie with Potato Pastry

The soft potato pastry is great for mopping
up the lovely cooking juices.

METHOD

Preheat the oven to 200°C/400°F/Gas Mark 6.

To make the filling, dust the chicken pieces with flour. Heat
some oil and butter in a frying pan, add the chicken and fry,
turning occasionally, until golden brown. Transfer to a shallow
casserole dish, add the tomatoes, parsley and chives and pour
in the Guinness. Cover with a layer of bacon and set aside while
you make the pastry.

Put the flour into a mixing bowl and rub in the butter. Add the
potatoes and salt and mix. Add the egg and mix well.

Turn out onto a work surface lightly dusted with flour and
knead until soft and elastic. Roll out the dough to a thickness of
2.5 cm/1 inch and place on top of the bacon.

Brush with milk and bake in the preheated oven for 20 minutes.
Reduce the oven temperature to 180°C/350°F/Gas Mark 4 and
cook for a further 30 minutes, or until the chicken is cooked
through. Serve hot.

SERVES 6

BISCUITS, BUNS, TARTLETS & TRAYBAKES

INGREDIENTS

225 g/8 oz porridge oats, plus extra for dusting

60 g/2¼ oz wholemeal flour, plus extra for dusting

½ tsp bicarbonate of soda

1 tsp salt

½ tsp sugar

85 g/3 oz butter, plus extra for greasing

4-5 tbsp hot water

Crunchy Savoury Oatcakes

These are very quick and easy to prepare and are delicious with any kind of cheese or with smoked fish.

METHOD

Preheat the oven to 190°C/375°F/Gas Mark 5. Grease a baking tray.

Put the oats, flour, bicarbonate of soda, salt and sugar into a bowl and mix to combine. Add the butter and rub it in until the mixture has the consistency of coarse breadcrumbs.

Gradually add the water and mix until the dough is thick but not sticky.

Roll out the dough to a thickness of 5 mm/¼ inch on a work surface lightly dusted with a mixture of oats and flour. Cut out 12 rounds with a biscuit cutter and place on the prepared tray.

Bake in the preheated oven for 20–30 minutes until golden. Leave to cool in the tray until firm, then transfer to a wire rack and leave to cool completely. Store in an airtight container.

MAKES 12

INGREDIENTS

350 g/12 oz self-raising flour

pinch of salt

200 g/7 oz demerara sugar

5-cm/2-inch piece fresh ginger, grated

1 tsp bicarbonate of soda

125 g/4½ oz butter, plus extra for greasing

75 g/2¾ oz golden syrup

1 egg, beaten

granulated sugar, for sprinkling

Ginger Nuts

These traditional biscuits have a lovely texture – fresh ginger adds extra spice.

METHOD

Preheat the oven to 160°C/325°F/Gas Mark 3. Lightly grease two large baking trays.

Sift the flour and salt into a mixing bowl, then stir in the demerara sugar, ginger and bicarbonate of soda.

Put the butter and golden syrup into a small saucepan and heat over a very low heat until the butter has melted. Leave to cool slightly.

Pour the butter mixture onto the dry ingredients, add the egg and mix to a firm dough. With damp hands, roll the dough into 30 walnut-sized balls and place on the prepared trays, well spaced to allow for spreading, then flatten slightly with your fingers. Sprinkle with a little granulated sugar.

Bake in the preheated oven for 15–20 minutes. Leave to cool in the trays for 5 minutes, or until just beginning to firm up, then transfer to wire racks and leave to cool completely.

MAKES 30

INGREDIENTS

90 g/3¼ oz plain flour

2 tbsp cocoa powder

115 g/4 oz butter, plus extra for greasing

55 g/2 oz caster sugar

½ tsp vanilla extract

Chocolate Biscuits

Nothing says 'treat' better than a chocolate biscuit with a cup of tea or coffee. These are simplicity itself to prepare.

METHOD

Preheat the oven to 190°C/375°F/Gas Mark 5. Lightly grease two large baking trays.

Sift the flour and cocoa powder together into a bowl. Put the butter, sugar and vanilla extract into a separate bowl and cream together until pale and fluffy.

Add the flour mixture to the butter mixture and stir until well combined. Drop teaspoons of the mixture on the prepared trays, well spaced to allow for spreading.

Bake in the preheated oven for 15–20 minutes until firm. Leave to cool in the trays for 1 minute, then transfer to wire racks and leave to cool completely.

MAKES 20

INGREDIENTS

125 g/4½ oz butter
55 g/2 oz caster sugar, plus extra for sprinkling
175 g/6 oz plain flour, plus extra for dusting

Shortbread Fingers

These crumbly, buttery fingers are incredibly easy to make, yet they never fail to impress.

METHOD

Preheat the oven to 190°C/375°F/Gas Mark 5. Line two large baking sheets with baking paper.

Put the butter and sugar into a mixing bowl and cream together until pale and smooth. Add the flour and stir to a smooth paste.

Turn out onto a work surface lightly dusted with flour and roll out to a thickness of 1 cm/½ inch. Cut into fingers and place on the prepared baking sheets. Sprinkle with sugar and chill in the fridge for 15 minutes.

Bake in the preheated oven for 15–20 minutes until golden. Transfer to a wire rack and leave to cool.

MAKES 24

INGREDIENTS

85 g/3 oz plain flour

½ tsp salt

115 g/4 oz porridge oats

70 g/2½ oz raisins, sultanas, dried cranberries or apricots

25 g/1 oz chopped walnuts, hazelnuts or cashew nuts

70 g/2½ oz soft light brown sugar

140 g/5 oz butter, plus extra for greasing

1 tsp golden syrup

½ tsp bicarbonate of soda

2 tbsp boiling water

2 tsp cider vinegar

Oaty Fruit & Nut Biscuits

These oaty biscuits are very quick to rustle up. The type of dried fruit and nuts you use is up to you.

METHOD

Preheat the oven to 180°C/350°F/Gas Mark 4 and grease a large baking tray.

Sift the flour and salt into a mixing bowl, add the oats, raisins, walnuts and sugar and stir to combine.

Put the butter and golden syrup into a small saucepan and heat until the butter is melted. Mix the bicarbonate of soda with the boiling water in a small cup.

Add the butter mixture to the dry ingredients, then add the bicarbonate of soda mixture and the vinegar. Mix thoroughly.

Drop teaspoons of the mixture onto the prepared tray and bake in the middle of the preheated oven for 25–30 minutes. Leave to cool in the tray for 5 minutes, then transfer to a wire rack and leave to cool completely.

MAKES 15-20

INGREDIENTS

225 g/8 oz butter, plus extra for greasing

225 g/8 oz caster sugar

2 tsp clear honey

4 tbsp hot water

225 g/8 oz rolled oats

225 g/8 oz plain flour

1 tsp baking powder

1 tsp bicarbonate of soda

Oat & Honey Crunch Biscuits

These crunchy, slightly chewy biscuits are perfect for eating with your morning coffee. Add a handful of chocolate chips along with the oats for a touch of luxury.

METHOD

Preheat the oven to 190°C/375°F/Gas Mark 5 and grease two large baking sheets.

Put the butter and sugar into a mixing bowl and cream until pale and fluffy. Add the honey and water and stir to combine.

Add the oats and sift in the flour, baking powder and bicarbonate of soda.

Mix well, then roll the mixture into walnut-sized balls with your hands and arrange on the prepared baking sheets, well spaced to allow for spreading.

Bake in the preheated oven for 10–15 minutes. Leave to cool on the baking sheets for 10 minutes, then transfer to wire racks and leave to cool completely.

Store in an airtight tin for up to 1 week.

MAKES ABOUT 30

INGREDIENTS

175 g/6 oz self-raising flour, plus extra for dusting

½ tsp bicarbonate of soda

125 g/4 oz butter, plus extra for greasing

2 tsp golden syrup

85 g/3 oz granulated sugar

Portarlington Golden Biscuits

A nice, plain eggless biscuit that you can rustle up from storecupboard ingredients.

METHOD

Preheat the oven to 200°C/400°F/Gas Mark 6 and grease a large baking tray.

Sift the flour and bicarbonate of soda together into a bowl.

Put the butter, golden syrup and sugar into a small saucepan and heat until the sugar is dissolved. Bring to the boil, then pour into the flour mixture and stir well to combine.

Dust your hands with flour and roll the mixture into walnut-sized balls. Place them on the prepared baking tray, well spaced to allow for spreading, and bake in the middle of the preheated oven for 10–15 minutes until golden. Leave to cool in the tray for 5 minutes, then transfer to a wire rack and leave to cool completely.

MAKES 15–20

INGREDIENTS

350 g/12 oz plain white flour

1 tsp cream of tartar

½ tsp bicarbonate of soda

225 g/8 oz butter, plus extra for greasing

225 g/8 oz caster sugar

1 egg, beaten

Porter Hope Biscuits

A great recipe for a biscuit tin standby.

METHOD

Preheat the oven to 180°C/350°F/Gas Mark 4 and grease two large baking trays.

Put the flour, cream of tartar and bicarbonate of soda into a bowl and mix to combine. Rub in the butter, then stir in the sugar. Add the egg and mix to a firm dough. Break off walnut-sized pieces of the dough, roll into balls and flatten onto the prepared trays using a fork. Space well to allow for spreading.

Bake in the middle of the preheated oven for 20 minutes (you will have to do this in batches), or until golden. Leave to cool in the trays for 5 minutes, then transfer to a wire rack and leave to cool completely.

MAKES 36

INGREDIENTS

175 g/6 oz self-raising flour

125 g/4½ oz caster sugar

125 g/4½ oz butter, softened

2 eggs, beaten

2 tbsp cold water

1 tsp vanilla extract

200 g/7 oz icing sugar

2 tbsp lukewarm water

liquid food colouring

hundreds and thousands, to decorate

Queen Cakes

Children love to help with baking and decorating these little cakes. They're very popular for afternoon tea and, of course, children's parties.

METHOD

Preheat the oven to 200°C/400°F/Gas Mark 6. Line two 8-hole bun tins with paper cases.

Put the flour, caster sugar, butter, eggs, cold water and vanilla extract into a bowl and beat until smooth. Fill the paper cases two-thirds full with the batter.

Bake in the preheated oven for about 15 minutes until golden, then remove from the tins, transfer to a wire rack and leave to cool completely.

Sift the icing sugar into a bowl and mix in enough of the lukewarm water to make a thick, smooth paste. Add a few drops of food colouring, then spread the icing over the cakes and sprinkle with hundreds and thousands.

MAKES 16

Baking with Oats & other Grains

In years gone by, wheat was a relatively expensive grain, and few Irish households could afford to use it regularly until the 20th century. However, good use was made of other grains.

Oats

Oaten bread will strengthen your arm. (Traditional Irish saying)

Oats grow well in the damp Irish climate and in poor soil conditions, so they were a good substitute for wheat flour.

They add body and texture to every kind of bake, from bread to muffins to flapjacks, and are used to add crunch to the toppings for crumbles and fruit tarts.

Barley

Barley is also grown in Ireland, although it is not so hardy a grain as oats, and is used in baking to some extent. Barley flour is a bit sweeter than wheat flour, but produces a similar texture when baked. It has enough gluten to be used as the main ingredient in biscuits and muffins, but will not hold a loaf of bread together and should always be used in conjunction with a stronger flour.

Rice

This is a not a native grain and is not greatly used in Irish baking, although nothing beats the comfort of a traditional creamy baked rice pudding, made with pearl rice.

Corn

Most people's idea of corn is sweetcorn, those golden kernels that can be added to soups and salads, or eaten directly off a grilled cob. While Italian polenta is now becoming popular, use of corn and its products in Ireland is generally limited to cornflour, which is a starch extracted from corn kernels and is useful mainly as a thickener in soups and stews. It can be used in baking to a limited extent – some shortbread recipes include it, and it can also be useful to add a little to soufflés, mousses and meringues.

INGREDIENTS

55 g/2 oz caster sugar

55 g/2 oz butter, softened, plus extra for greasing

1 egg, beaten

½ tsp bicarbonate of soda

½ tsp salt

175 g/6 oz porridge oats

Sweet Oatcakes

This is the basic Irish sweet biscuit – the only grain used is oats.

METHOD

Preheat the oven to 200°C/400°F/Gas Mark 6. Grease a large baking sheet.

Put the sugar and butter into a bowl and cream until pale and fluffy. Add the egg and beat to combine. Add the bicarbonate of soda, salt and oats and mix to combine.

Shape into walnut-sized balls and place on the prepared baking sheet, well spaced to allow for spreading. Bake in the preheated oven for 20 minutes until browned on top.

MAKES ABOUT 20

INGREDIENTS

125 g/4½ oz plain white flour

1 tsp baking powder

200 g/7 oz soft light brown sugar

75 g/2¾ oz desiccated coconut

125 g/4½ oz butter, melted, plus extra for greasing

Topping

400 ml/14 fl oz sweetened condensed milk

25 g/1 oz butter

150 g/6 oz dried dates, chopped

2 tbsp golden syrup

55 g/2 oz hazelnuts, chopped

Sticky Date Fingers

These indulgent bites are perfect for tea on a cold winter's afternoon.

METHOD

Preheat the oven to 180°C/350°F/Gas Mark 4. Grease a 20 x 30-cm/8 x 12-inch traybake tin and line with baking paper.

Put the flour, baking powder, sugar and coconut into a bowl and mix to combine. Stir in the butter and mix well. Press the mixture into the base of the prepared tin and bake in the preheated oven for 15 minutes, or until firm.

Meanwhile, to make the topping, put all the ingredients except the nuts into a small saucepan and heat over a low heat, stirring constantly, until golden brown. Spread the topping over the base, sprinkle over the nuts and return to the oven for a further 10 minutes.

Leave to cool, then cut into 16 fingers and remove from the tin to serve.

MAKES 16

INGREDIENTS

175 g/6 oz self-raising flour

125 g/4½ oz caster sugar

125 g/4½ oz butter

2 eggs, beaten

2 tbsp cold water

1 tsp vanilla extract

5 tbsp strawberry or raspberry jam

5 tbsp whipped cream

icing sugar, for dusting

Butterfly Cakes

These impressive-looking cakes are incredibly easy to make and are a very popular tea-time treat.

METHOD

Preheat the oven to 200°C/400°F/Gas Mark 6. Line two 8-hole bun tins with paper cases.

Put the flour, caster sugar, butter, eggs, water and vanilla extract into a bowl and beat until smooth. Fill the paper cases two-thirds full with the batter.

Bake in the preheated oven for about 15 minutes until golden, then remove from the tins, transfer to a wire rack and leave to cool completely.

Cut the tops off the cakes and set aside. Put a teaspoon of jam and a teaspoon of cream on top of each cake, then cut the reserved pieces in half and place two halves on each cake, set at an angle to imitate wings.

Dust with icing sugar just before serving.

MAKES 16

INGREDIENTS

175 g/6 oz self-raising flour

125 g/4½ oz caster sugar

3 tbsp cocoa powder

125 g/4½ oz butter

2 eggs, beaten

2 tbsp cold water

1 tsp vanilla extract

1 tbsp icing sugar, plus extra for dusting

5 tbsp whipped cream

Chocolate Butterfly Cakes

This luxurious version of the butterfly cake combines chocolate with cream.

METHOD

Preheat the oven to 200°C/400°F/Gas Mark 6. Line two 8-hole bun tins with paper cases.

Put the flour, caster sugar, cocoa powder, butter, eggs, water and vanilla extract into a bowl and beat until smooth. Fill the paper cases two-thirds full with the batter.

Bake in the preheated oven for about 15 minutes until golden, then remove from the tins, transfer to a wire rack and leave to cool completely.

Cut the tops off the cakes and set aside. Mix the icing sugar with the cream and put a teaspoon of the mixture on each cake. Cut the reserved pieces in half and place two halves on each cake, set at an angle to represent wings.

Dust with icing sugar just before serving.

MAKES 16

INGREDIENTS

175 g/6 oz self-raising flour, plus extra for dusting

85 g/3 oz chilled butter, plus extra for greasing

100 g/3½ oz jam

milk, for brushing

Jam Tarts

Every child's favourite, these delicious little tarts can be made with whatever type of jam you prefer. Resist the temptation to eat them straight out of the oven – the jam will be extremely hot.

METHOD

Preheat the oven to 200°C/400°F/Gas Mark 6. Grease 20 holes in two bun tins.

Put the flour into a mixing bowl, cut in the butter and rub it in until fine crumbs form. Add a few spoons of water and mix to a firm dough.

Roll out the dough on a work surface lightly dusted with flour and cut out 20 rounds with a 9-cm/3½-inch fluted cutter.

Ease the pastry rounds into the prepared tins and place a teaspoon of jam in each round.

Re-roll the pastry trimmings, cut out stars or other shapes and place these on the tarts. Brush the pastry with milk and bake the tarts in the preheated oven for 20–30 minutes until golden.

Leave to cool in the tins for 10 minutes, then turn out onto a wire rack and leave to cool until you're ready to serve them.

MAKES 20

INGREDIENTS

butter, for greasing

350 g/12 oz self-raising flour

125 g/4½ oz white vegetable fat

1 tsp mixed spice

1 tsp ground ginger

85 g/3 oz demerara or soft light brown sugar

1 egg, beaten

1 tbsp milk

Spiced Buns

These tasty buns were traditionally made with beef dripping, but white vegetable fat makes a good substitute and gives them a great texture.

METHOD

Preheat the oven to 180°C/350°F/Gas Mark 4. Grease a large baking tray.

Put the flour into a mixing bowl and cut in the vegetable fat, rubbing it in with your fingertips until fine crumbs form. Add the mixed spice, ginger and sugar and stir to combine. Add the egg and enough milk to make a soft but not wet dough.

Divide the dough into about 20 equal pieces and shape each piece into a bun. Place the buns on the prepared tray and bake in the preheated oven for 15–20 minutes until golden. Serve warm or cold.

MAKES 20-24

INGREDIENTS

4 egg whites

pinch of salt

125 g/4½ oz granulated sugar

125 g/4½ oz caster sugar

300 ml/10 fl oz double cream, whipped

melted plain chocolate or strawberry sauce, for drizzling

Meringues

These are an afternoon tea favourite – they also make a great dessert, drizzled with melted chocolate or strawberry sauce.

METHOD

Preheat the oven to 120°C/250°F/Gas Mark ½ and line two large baking trays with baking paper.

Whisk the egg whites with the salt in a large grease-free bowl until they hold stiff peaks.

Gradually whisk in the granulated sugar – the meringue will begin to look glossy. Gradually add the caster sugar, whisking until the meringue is thick and holds stiff peaks.

Put the mixture into a piping bag fitted with a 2.5-cm/1-inch star nozzle and pipe 12 whirls onto each of the prepared trays.

Bake in the preheated oven until the meringues have a golden tinge and can be lifted off the paper easily. Switch off the oven and leave the meringues inside for 8 hours.

To serve, sandwich pairs of meringues together with a large spoonful of whipped cream, arrange on a serving plate and drizzle with melted chocolate.

MAKES 12

INGREDIENTS

275 g/9¾ oz white self-raising flour

150 g/5½ oz butter, softened, plus extra for greasing

150 g/5½ oz soft light brown sugar

1 tsp ground cinnamon

1 cooking apple, grated

1 egg, beaten

1 tbsp milk

caster sugar, for sprinkling

Apple Fingers

These spongy cakes make a great lunchbox treat, or can be heated up and served with custard or cream for dessert.

METHOD

Preheat the oven to 200°C/400·F/Gas Mark 6 and grease a Swiss roll tin.

Put the flour into a mixing bowl, add the butter, brown sugar, cinnamon and apple and mix well to combine.

Add the egg and milk and mix to a soft dough. Spread the dough in the prepared tin and bake in the preheated oven for 30 minutes, turning the tin halfway through the baking time.

Transfer the tin to a wire rack, sprinkle with caster sugar and mark the cake into 12 fingers with a knife. Leave to cool in the tin, then cut the fingers along the marks. Place the tin on a wire rack and leave to cool for a further 30 minutes before removing the fingers.

MAKES 12

INGREDIENTS

350 g/12 oz rolled oats

175 g/6 oz demerara sugar

pinch of salt

225 g/8 oz butter, plus extra for greasing

2 tbsp golden syrup

Flapjacks

These are a classic family favourite and are very easy to make. They can be stored in an airtight tin for up to two weeks.

METHOD

Preheat the oven to 180°C/325°F/Gas Mark 4. Grease a baking tray.

Put the oats, sugar and salt into a mixing bowl and mix to combine.

Put the butter and golden syrup into a saucepan and heat over a medium heat until the butter is melted.

Pour the butter mixture over the dry ingredients and mix well. Press the mixture into the prepared tray, then bake in the preheated oven for 30 minutes.

Leave to cool in the tray for about 10 minutes, then cut into squares, transfer to a wire rack and leave to cool completely.

MAKES ABOUT 24

INGREDIENTS

100 g/3½ oz
porridge oats
25 g/1 oz plain flour
55 g/2 oz ground
almonds
pinch of salt
85 g/3 oz butter,
melted, plus extra
for greasing
1 tsp almond extract
1 tbsp golden syrup,
plus extra if needed
3 tbsp raspberry jam
flaked almonds, to
decorate

Bakewell Flapjacks

A combination of two traditional family favourites, flapjacks and Bakewell tart, these are sure to become a regular weekend bake.

METHOD

Preheat the oven to 160°C/325°F/Gas Mark 3 and grease a 14-cm/5½-inch square baking tin.

Put the oats, flour, ground almonds and salt into a mixing bowl and stir to combine. Add the butter, almond extract and golden syrup and mix well, adding a little more syrup if the mixture is too dry to come together.

Spread half the mixture in the base of the prepared tin and level using the back of a wet spoon. Spread the jam evenly over this layer, leaving a 5-mm/¼-inch border. Spread the remaining oat mixture on top and sprinkle with flaked almonds.

Bake in the preheated oven for 15–20 minutes. It will start to brown very quickly towards the end of the cooking time, so keep an eye on it to prevent burning.

Leave to cool in the tin for 10 minutes, then use a sharp knife to mark into 8 bars. Leave to cool for a further 20 minutes, then carefully remove from the tin, transfer to a wire rack and leave to cool completely.

MAKES 8

INGREDIENTS

225 g/8 oz ready-
to-eat dried apricots,
finely chopped

1 tbsp clear honey

5 tbsp water

1 tbsp lemon juice

1 tsp ground
cinnamon

175 g/6 oz butter,
softened, plus extra
for greasing

85 g/3 oz caster
sugar

175 g/6 oz semolina

175 g/6 oz
wholemeal self-
raising flour

Fruit Slices

You can use any dried fruit for these,
but apricots are particularly tangy and
delicious.

METHOD

Preheat the oven to 160°C/325°F/Gas Mark 3 and grease a 28 x
20-cm/11 x 8-inch deep baking tin.

Put the apricots, honey, water and lemon juice into a saucepan
and heat over a low heat, stirring until the honey has dissolved
and the mixture is creamy. Remove from the heat and set aside
until needed.

Put the butter and sugar into a mixing bowl and cream together
until pale and fluffy, then add the semolina and flour and stir
until the mixture comes together and is crumbly in texture.

Spread half the flour mixture in the prepared tin, pushing it
into the corners, then spread the apricot mixture on top. Finish
with the remaining flour mixture, levelling the top, then bake in
the preheated oven for 40–45 minutes until golden.

Leave to cool in the tin for 10 minutes, then use a sharp knife
to mark into 16 bars. Leave in the tin for a further 20 minutes,
then carefully remove, transfer to a wire rack and leave to cool
completely.

MAKES 16

INGREDIENTS

125 g/4½ plain flour, plus extra for dusting

pinch of salt

180 g/6¼ oz butter, plus extra for greasing

125 g/4½ oz caster sugar

1 egg, beaten

175 g/6 oz porridge oats

2 tbsp apricot jam

Apricot Oat Fingers

These crumbly slices have a tangy layer of apricot jam.

METHOD

Preheat the oven to 220°C/425°F/Gas Mark 7 and grease a Swiss roll tin.

Sift the flour and salt into a mixing bowl, then rub in 55 g/2 oz of the butter until fine crumbs form. Add enough water to mix to a firm dough and mix it in with a knife. Set aside until needed.

Put the remaining butter into a saucepan and heat until melted. Remove from the heat and stir in the sugar and egg, then add the oats and mix well.

Turn out the dough onto a work surface lightly dusted with flour and roll out thinly. Use to line the prepared tin. Spread the jam on top, then cover with the oat mixture, levelling the surface. Bake in the preheated oven for 20–30 minutes until light brown on top.

Leave to cool in the tin for 10 minutes, then use a sharp knife to mark into 12 slices. Leave in the tin for a further 20 minutes, then remove the fingers, transfer to a wire rack and leave to cool completely.

MAKES 12

INGREDIENTS

225 g/8 oz plain flour
pinch of salt
1 tsp baking powder
85 g/3 oz butter, plus extra for greasing
85 g/3 oz caster sugar
55 g/2 oz desiccated coconut
1 egg, beaten
150 ml/5 fl oz milk

Coconut Biscuits

Coconut gives a tropical flavour to an ordinary plain biscuit.

METHOD

Preheat the oven to 200°C/400°F/Gas Mark 6 and grease a large baking tray.

Sift the flour, salt and baking powder into a mixing bowl, then rub in the butter until fine crumbs form. Add the sugar and coconut and mix well to combine.

Add the egg and milk and mix to a stiff batter. Drop 12 mounds of the batter onto the prepared tray, well spaced to allow for spreading.

Bake in the preheated oven for 15–20 minutes until golden. Transfer to a wire rack and leave to cool.

MAKES 12

INGREDIENTS

225 g/8 oz self-raising flour

125 g/4½ oz butter, plus extra for greasing

85 g/3 oz caster sugar

125 g/4½ oz mixed dried fruit

1 egg, beaten

2 tbsp milk

granulated sugar, for sprinkling

Rock Buns

The classic everyday bun – great with a cup of tea or coffee.

METHOD

Preheat the oven to 200°C/400°F/Gas Mark 6 and grease a large baking tray.

Sift the flour into a mixing bowl, then rub in the butter until fine crumbs form. Add the caster sugar and dried fruit and mix well to combine.

Add the egg and milk and mix to a stiff batter. Drop 12 mounds of the batter onto the prepared tray, well spaced to allow for spreading.

Sprinkle the buns with granulated sugar and bake in the preheated oven for 10–15 minutes until golden. Leave to cool in the tin for 5 minutes, then transfer to a wire rack and leave to cool completely.

MAKES 12

FESTIVE BAKES

INGREDIENTS

1 kg/2 lb 4 oz mixed dried fruit, including cherries or cranberries

juice and grated zest of 1 orange

juice and grated zest of 1 lemon

150 ml/5 fl oz Irish whiskey, plus extra for feeding

250 g/9 oz butter, softened

200 g/7 oz soft light brown sugar

175 g/6 oz plain flour

½ tsp baking powder

100 g/3½ oz ground almonds

100 g/3½ oz flaked almonds

2 tsp mixed spice

1 tsp ground cinnamon

½ tsp ground cloves

4 large eggs, beaten

1 tsp almond extract

SERVES 12–15

Christmas Cake

This traditional Christmas cake is 'fed' with whiskey over a period of weeks. Make it at least 6 weeks in advance.

METHOD

Put the dried fruit, orange juice and zest, lemon juice and zest, whiskey, butter and sugar into a large saucepan and bring to the boil over a medium heat. Reduce the heat and simmer for 5 minutes. Transfer the contents of the pan to a large mixing bowl and leave to stand for 30 minutes.

Preheat the oven to 150°C/300°F/Gas Mark 2. Line a large cake tin with a double layer of baking paper and wrap a double layer of brown paper around the tin, securing it with kitchen string.

Add the flour, baking powder, ground almonds, flaked almonds, mixed spice, cinnamon, cloves, eggs and almond extract to the fruit mixture and stir until well combined. Tip into the prepared tin, level the top and bake in the centre of the preheated oven for 2 hours.

Remove from the oven and prick all over with a skewer or knitting needle, then slowly pour 2–3 tablespoons of whiskey over the cake, allowing it to soak in. Leave to cool completely in the tin, then turn out, peel off the baking paper and wrap the cake in foil. Repeat the whiskey feeding procedure every 2 weeks, allowing the cake to dry out for a week before icing it.

INGREDIENTS

200 g/7 oz plain flour, plus extra for dusting

100 g/3½ oz chilled butter

25 g/1 oz icing sugar, plus extra for dusting

1 egg yolk, beaten

2–3 tbsp milk

300 g/10½ oz ready-made mincemeat

1 egg, beaten, for glazing

Mince Pies

Nothing says Christmas quite like a mince pie. It was once traditional to make your own mincemeat, but there are now some very good ready-made ones available.

METHOD

Preheat the oven to 180°C/350°F/Gas Mark 4. Dust a 12-hole tartlet tin with flour, shaking out any excess.

Sift the flour into a mixing bowl and rub in the butter until fine crumbs form. Add the sugar and egg yolk and stir in enough milk to mix to a soft dough. Turn out onto a work surface lightly dusted with flour and knead until smooth.

Shape into a ball and roll out to a thickness of 1 cm/½ inch. Cut out 12 rounds with a 7-cm/2¾-inch cutter and use to line the prepared tin.

Prick the bases with a fork and add a large spoon of mincemeat to each pie. Roll out the pastry trimmings, cut out large stars or Christmas trees and use to decorate the pies.

Brush with beaten egg and bake in the preheated oven for 15 minutes. Leave to cool in the tin for 10 minutes, then transfer to a wire rack and leave to cool completely. Dust with icing sugar just before serving.

MAKES 12

INGREDIENTS

butter, for greasing

100 g/3½ oz plain flour

2 tsp ground cinnamon

2 tsp mixed spice

2 tsp ground nutmeg

350 g/12 oz fresh breadcrumbs

55 g/2 oz ground almonds

675 g/1 lb 8 oz mixed sultanas, raisins and currants

100 g/3½ oz glacé cherries, chopped

175 g/6 oz chopped mixed peel

juice and grated zest of 1 lemon

juice and grated zest of 1 orange

25 g/8 oz grated suet

5 eggs, beaten

300 ml/10 fl oz Guinness

4 tbsp dark rum

MAKES 2 PUDDINGS

Baked Christmas Pudding

This method of cooking the Christmas pudding means you can happily leave it in the oven without worrying about topping up the cooking water on the hob.

METHOD

Preheat the oven to 150°C/300°F/Gas Mark 2. Grease two 1.2-litre/2-pint pudding basins.

Put the flour, cinnamon, mixed spice, nutmeg, breadcrumbs, almonds, mixed dried fruit, glacé cherries and mixed peel into a large mixing bowl and mix to combine. Make a well in the centre and add the lemon juice and zest, orange juice and zest and suet and mix well.

Add the eggs and mix well, then pour in the Guinness and rum and mix thoroughly. Divide the batter between the prepared basins and cover with a double layer of greaseproof paper and a layer of foil, securing with kitchen string.

Put the puddings into a roasting tin and add hot water until the tin is three-quarters full. Bake in the preheated oven for 6 hours.

INGREDIENTS

butter, for greasing
3 eggs
85 g/3 oz caster
sugar
80 g/2¾ oz plain
flour
½ tsp baking powder
2 tbsp cocoa powder
holly sprig, to
decorate

Frosting

55 g/2 oz butter
150 g/5½ oz plain
chocolate
1 tbsp golden syrup
75 ml/2½ fl oz
double cream
200 g/7 oz icing
sugar, sifted, plus
extra for dusting

Filling

225 ml/8 fl oz
double cream

SERVES 8

Yule Log

This luscious chocolate cake is a big Christmas favourite with children.

METHOD

Preheat the oven to 200°C/400°F/Gas Mark 6. Grease a Swiss roll tin and line with baking paper. Put the eggs and caster sugar into a bowl and whisk for 10 minutes, or until thick and creamy.

Mix the flour, baking powder and cocoa powder together in a bowl, then sift into the egg and sugar mixture. Fold in very gently, then pour the mixture into the prepared tin, tipping it slightly so that the mixture goes right into the corners. Bake in the preheated oven for 10 minutes. Leave to cool in the tin for 10 minutes, then invert onto a sheet of baking paper. Peel off the lining paper and roll up the cake from a long edge, using the paper to help – the paper will be inside the rolled-up cake. Leave to cool.

To make the frosting, put the butter and chocolate into a heatproof bowl set over a saucepan of gently simmering water and heat until melted. Remove from the heat, stir in the golden syrup and cream, then beat in the icing sugar until smooth.

To make the filling, whip the cream until it holds soft peaks, then unroll the cake, remove the paper and spread with the cream before rolling it up again.

Spread the frosting over the cake and score lines in it with a fork so that it looks like tree bark. Decorate with a holly sprig and serve.

INGREDIENTS

100 g/3½ oz
butter, plus extra for
greasing

100 g/3½ oz caster
sugar

1 egg yolk

½ tsp vanilla extract

150 g/5 oz plain
flour, plus extra for
dusting

55 g/2 oz ground
almonds

½ tsp mixed spice

Christmas Stars

These pretty little biscuits can be
decorated however you like. You can hang
them from the Christmas tree on ribbons
if you pierce a hole in one point of each
star with a skewer before baking.

METHOD

Preheat the oven to 180°C/350°F/Gas Mark 4. Grease two large
baking sheets.

Put the butter and sugar into a mixing bowl and cream together
until pale and fluffy. Beat in the egg yolk and the vanilla extract.
Add the flour, almonds and mixed spice and mix to a stiff
dough.

Turn out the dough onto a work surface lightly dusted with
flour and knead lightly. Roll out to a thickness of 5 mm/¼ inch
and use a star-shaped cutter to cut out biscuits.

Carefully transfer the biscuits to the prepared baking sheets and
bake in the preheated oven for 12–15 minutes until golden.
Leave to cool on the baking sheets for 1–2 minutes, then
transfer to a wire rack and leave to cool completely.

MAKES 15–20

INGREDIENTS

450 g/1 lb plain flour

½ tsp freshly grated nutmeg

pinch of salt

15 g/½ oz fresh yeast

55 g/2 oz soft light brown sugar

300 ml/10 fl oz lukewarm milk

2 eggs, beaten

55 g/2 oz butter, plus extra for greasing

115 g/4 oz mixed peel

225 g/8 oz currants

225 g/8 oz raisins

1 egg yolk, beaten, for glazing

Barm Brack

Made with yeast, this traditional Halloween treat is a sweet bread rather than a cake.

METHOD

Grease a 20-cm/8-inch round cake tin. Sift the flour, nutmeg and salt into a large mixing bowl.

In a separate bowl, blend the yeast with 1 teaspoon of the sugar and a little of the milk until it froths.

Add the remaining sugar to the flour mixture. Add the remaining milk to the yeast mixture, then add to the flour with the eggs and butter. Mix with a wooden spoon for about 10 minutes until stiff.

Fold in the mixed peel, currants and raisins, then transfer the batter to the prepared tin. Cover with a damp tea towel and leave to rise for about 1 hour until doubled in size.

Meanwhile, preheat the oven to 200°C/400°F/Gas Mark 6. Bake the brack in the preheated oven for 1 hour, then glaze with the beaten egg yolk and bake for a further 5 minutes. Leave to cool in the tin for 10 minutes, then turn out onto a wire rack and leave to cool completely.

SERVES 10–12

INGREDIENTS

oil, for brushing

500 g/1 lb 2 oz strong white flour, plus extra for dusting

½ tsp salt

2 tsp mixed spice

1 tsp ground nutmeg

1 tsp ground cinnamon

2 tsp easy-blend yeast

55 g/2 oz golden caster sugar, plus extra for glazing

grated zest of 1 lemon

175 g/6 oz currants

85 g/3 oz chopped mixed peel

85 g/3 oz butter, melted

1 egg, beaten

225 ml/8 fl oz lukewarm milk, plus extra cold milk for glazing

Pastry crosses

55 g/2 oz plain flour

25 g/1 oz chilled butter, diced

1 tbsp cold water

MAKES 12

Hot Cross Buns

Traditionally eaten on Good Friday, these sticky spiced buns are now a favourite throughout Lent. The crosses are optional.

METHOD

Brush a baking sheet and a bowl with oil. Sift the flour, salt and spices into a mixing bowl. Stir in the yeast, sugar, lemon zest, currants and peel. Make a well in the centre. Put the butter, egg and milk into a separate bowl and mix to combine. Pour into the dry ingredients and mix to a soft dough. Turn out onto a work surface lightly dusted with flour and knead for 10 minutes until smooth. Place in the oiled bowl, cover with clingfilm and set aside in a warm place for up to 2 hours, or until doubled in volume.

Turn out the dough and knead for 2 minutes. Shape into 12 balls and place on the prepared baking sheet. Cover with oiled clingfilm and set aside in a warm place for 45 minutes. Meanwhile, preheat the oven to 220°C/425°F/Gas Mark 7.

To make the pastry crosses, sift the flour into a bowl, rub in the butter and stir in the water to mix to a dough. Roll it into 24 strips, each 18 cm/7 inches. Put 3 tablespoons of milk and 3 tablespoons of sugar into a saucepan and heat until the sugar is dissolved. Brush the glaze over the buns and lay two pastry strips on each of them in a cross shape. Bake in the preheated oven for 15–20 minutes until golden. Transfer to a wire rack and leave to cool.

Simple Simnel Cake

INGREDIENTS

175 g/6 oz butter, plus extra for greasing

175 g/6 oz caster sugar

3 large eggs, beaten

350 g/12 oz mixed currants and sultanas

55 g/2 oz chopped mixed peel

grated zest of 1 orange

grated zest of 1 lemon

225 g/8 oz self-raising flour

1 tsp mixed spice

3 tbsp brandy

Topping

450 g/1 lb marzipan

2 tsp apricot jam

1 egg, beaten

SERVES 10

Simnel cakes were made by young women in domestic service and given to their mothers on Mothering Sunday. The cakes were usually kept until Easter (Mothering Sunday often fell during Lent) and they have become a modern Easter tradition.

METHOD

Preheat the oven to 150°C/300°F/Gas Mark 2. Grease a 20-cm/8-inch round cake tin.

Put the butter and sugar into a mixing bowl and cream together until pale and fluffy. Gradually add the eggs, beating well after each addition. Fold in the mixed dried fruit, mixed peel, orange zest and lemon zest.

Sift in the flour and mixed spice and, using a metal spoon, fold in very carefully with the brandy. Spoon the batter into the prepared tin and level the top. Bake in the preheated oven for 2½–3 hours. Leave to cool in the tin for 15 minutes, then turn out onto a wire rack and leave to cool completely.

Meanwhile, make the topping. Roll out the marzipan and cut into a 20-cm/8-inch round. Brush the top of the cake with the jam and place the marzipan round on top. Using the marzipan trimmings, roll out 11 balls and place these around the edge of the topping. Brush with beaten egg and place under a medium grill until toasted.

INGREDIENTS

200 g/7 oz butter, plus extra for greasing

200 g/7 oz caster sugar

3 eggs, beaten

grated zest of 2 large lemons

200 g/7 oz self-raising flour, plus extra for dusting

candied lemon slices and mini chocolate eggs, to decorate

Filling and frosting

150 g/5½ oz icing sugar, plus extra for dusting

85 g/3 oz butter, softened

½ tsp lemon extract

SERVES 10

Easter Lemon Sponge

This light-textured, zesty cake will help offset all that Easter chocolate!

METHOD

Preheat the oven to 180°C/350°F/Gas Mark 4. Grease a 20-cm/8-inch round cake tin and dust with flour, shaking out any excess.

Put the butter and sugar into a mixing bowl and cream together until pale and fluffy. Gradually add the eggs, beating well after each addition. Add the lemon zest, stirring to incorporate.

Sift in the flour and, using a metal spoon, fold in until combined. Spoon the batter into the prepared tin and level the top. Bake in the preheated oven for 30–40 minutes until golden and a skewer inserted into the centre of he cake comes out clean. Leave to cool in the tin for 15 minutes, then turn out onto a wire rack and leave to cool completely.

Meanwhile, make the filling and frosting. Put the icing sugar and butter into a bowl and cream together until pale and fluffy. Add the lemon extract, then chill in the fridge until the cake is completely cooled.

Cut the cake in half horizontally. Spread two-thirds of the filling mixture on one half, then place the other half on top. Spread the remaining mixture on top, then dust with icing sugar and decorate with candied lemon slices and mini chocolate eggs.

INGREDIENTS

175 g/6 oz butter, softened, plus extra for greasing

175 g/6 oz caster sugar, plus extra for sprinkling

1 egg, beaten

1 tbsp milk

55 g/2 oz chopped mixed peel

115 g/4 oz currants or dried cherries

350 g/12 oz plain flour, plus extra for dusting

1 tsp mixed spice

1 egg white, beaten

Easter Biscuits

A traditional Easter biscuit, this recipe makes the most of all the ingredients that were forbidden during the Lenten season.

METHOD

Preheat the oven to 180°C/350°F/Gas Mark 4. Grease two large baking sheets. Put the butter and sugar into a mixing bowl and cream together until pale and fluffy. Gradually beat in the egg and milk, then stir in the mixed peel and currants.

Sift in the flour and mixed spice and mix to a firm dough. Knead until smooth, then turn out onto a work surface lightly dusted with flour and roll out to a thickness of 5 mm/¼ inch. Cut out 24 rounds with a 5-cm/2-inch round fluted cutter, rerolling and using the trimmings. Place the biscuits on the prepared baking sheets and bake in the preheated oven for 10 minutes until golden.

Remove from the oven – do not switch off the oven – and brush with the egg white. Sprinkle with sugar and return to the oven for 5 minutes. Leave to cool on the baking sheets for 2 minutes, then transfer to wire racks and leave to cool completely.

MAKES 24

For permission to reproduce copyright photographs, the publisher gratefully acknowledges the following:

p1 Shutterstock /A Fanfo
p2 Shutterstock / Tatyana Malova
p7 Flickr
p11 Paul Brookfield
p12 Shutterstock / Joy Brown
p15 Shutterstock / Janet Moore
p17 Shutterstock / Leigh Boardman
p19 Shutterstock / Axel Bueckert
p21 Shutterstock / Tatuasha
p23 National Museum of Ireland
p25 National Museum of Ireland
p27 Ben Potter
p29 Shutterstock / AnjelikaGr
p31 Shutterstock / Lucie Peclova
p33 Shutterstock / Laura Adamache
p35 Ben Potter
p37 Ben Potter
p39 Ben Potter
p41 Ben Potter
p43 Ben Potter
p45 Shutterstock / Olepeshkina
p47 Ben Potter
p49 Ben Potter
p52 Shutterstock / Lunasee Studios
p53 Shutterstock / Janet Moore
p55 Ben Potter
p57 Ben Potter
p59 Ben Potter
p61 Ben Potter
p63 Ben Potter
p64 Shutterstock / Pinkyone
p67 Shutterstock / Joerg Beuge

p69 Shutterstock / Thomas M Perkins
p71 Shutterstock / Monkeybusiness Images
p73 Shutterstock / G Aito
p75 Ben Potter
p77 Shutterstock / MShev
p79 Shutterstock / Pitamaha
p81 Shutterstock / Kostrez
p83 Shutterstock / RA3M
p85 Shutterstock / D Pimborough
p87 Shutterstock / AG Creations
p91 Ben Potter
p93 Ben Potter
p95 Shutterstock / Istetiana
p97 Ben Potter
p99 Shutterstock / Chris Smudge
p101 Shutterstock / Lesya Dolyuk
p103 Ben Potter
p105 Shutterstock / Joerg Beuge
p107 Shutterstock / Geshas
p109 Shutterstock / Lesya Dolyuk
p111 Ben Potter
p113 Shutterstock / Africa Studio
p115 Shutterstock / 2xDP
p117 Shutterstock / M Shev
p119 Shutterstock / AG Creations
p121 Shutterstock / Ingrid HS
p122 Shutterstock / Tyler W. Stipp
p125 Ben Potter
p127 Shutterstock / Anna Shepulova
p129 Shutterstock / Alexey Borodin
p131 Shutterstock / hlphoto

p133 Shutterstock / Tetiana Shumbasova
p135 Shutterstock / Monkey Business Images
p137 Shutterstock / Charles Brutlag
p141 Shutterstock / Catherine Jones
p143 Ben Potter
p145 Ben Potter
p147 Shutterstock / Amy Kerkemeyer
p149 Shutterstock / studiogi
p151 Shutterstock / MS Photographic
p153 Ben Potter
p155 Shutterstock / Gresei
p157 Shutterstock / YukikaeB
p159 Shutterstock / Shmeliova Natalia
p161 Shutterstock / M Shev
p163 Ben Potter
p165 Shutterstock / Foodio
p167 Shutterstock / Yulia-Bogdanova
p169 Shutterstock / Monkey Business Images
p171 Ben Potter
p173 Ben Potter
p175 Shutterstock / The Food Photographer
p177 Ben Potter
p179 Shutterstock / Margouillat
p181 Shutterstock / Elzbieta Sekowska
p183 Ben Potter
p184 Shutterstock / Andrey Solovev
p187 Shutterstock / Kiian Oksana
p189 Shutterstock / Marie C Fields
p191 Shutterstock / AS Food

p193 Ben Potter
p195 Shutterstock / CookieNim
p197 Shutterstock / Dream
p199 Shutterstock / Moving Moment
p201 Shutterstock / CatchaSnap
p203 Shutterstock / Kitch Bain
p205 Shutterstock / Alexei Novikov
p207 Shutterstock / Shtukicrew
p209 Ben Potter
p211 Shutterstock / M Shev
p213 Ben Potter
p215 Ben Potter
p217 Ben Potter
p219 Shutterstock / Denis Film
p221 Ben Potter
p223 Shutterstock / Merc
p225 Ben Potter
p227 Ben Potter
p229 Ben Potter
p231 Ben Potter
p233 Shutterstock / D Pimborough
p234 Shutterstock Lili Graphie
p237 Shutterstock / Joerg Beuge
p239 Shutterstock / Magdanatka
p241 Shutterstock / bitt
p243 Shutterstock / Lilyana Vynogradova
p245 Shutterstock / Kati Molin
p247 Shutterstock / Monkey Business Images
p249 Shutterstock / MS Photographic
p251 Shutterstock / Zoryanchik
p253 Ben Potter
p255 Shutterstock / Sarah Marchant